The City

Uwe Prell

The City

An Interdisciplinary Introduction
to Urban Studies

Translated from the German by Laura Radosh
English version fully revised and edited by Ute Reusch

Verlag Barbara Budrich
Opladen • Berlin • Toronto 2022

All rights reserved. No part of this publication may be reproduced, stored in or introduced into a retrieval system, or transmitted, in any form, or by any means (electronic, mechanical, photocopying, recording or otherwise) without the prior written permission of Verlag Barbara Budrich. Any person who does any unauthorized act in relation to this publication may be liable to criminal prosecution and civil claims for damages.

You must not circulate this book in any other binding or cover and you must impose this same condition on any acquirer.

A CIP catalogue record for this book is available from
Die Deutsche Bibliothek (The German Library)

© 2022 by Verlag Barbara Budrich GmbH, Opladen, Berlin & Toronto
www.budrich.eu

 ISBN 978-3-8474-2612-7 (Paperback)
 eISBN 978-3-8474-1771-2 (PDF)
 DOI   10.3224/84742612

Das Werk einschließlich aller seiner Teile ist urheberrechtlich geschützt. Jede Verwertung außerhalb der engen Grenzen des Urheberrechtsgesetzes ist ohne Zustimmung des Verlages unzulässig und strafbar. Das gilt insbesondere für Vervielfältigungen, Übersetzungen, Mikroverfilmungen und die Einspeicherung und Verarbeitung in elektronischen Systemen.

Die Deutsche Bibliothek – CIP-Einheitsaufnahme
Ein Titeldatensatz für die Publikation ist bei der Deutschen Bibliothek erhältlich.

Verlag Barbara Budrich GmbH
Stauffenbergstr. 7. D-51379 Leverkusen Opladen, Germany

86 Delma Drive. Toronto, ON M8W 4P6 Canada
www.budrich.eu

Jacket illustration by Bettina Lehfeldt, Kleinmachnow, Germany – www.lehfeldtgraphic.de
Cover image by Uwe Prell
Translated by Laura Radosh
English version fully revised and edited by Ute Reusch – www.englishagency.de
Typesetting by Ulrike Weingärtner, Gründau, Germany – info@textakzente.de
Printed in Europe on acid-free paper by paper & tinta, Warsaw

THE CITY IS THE ANSWER.
BUT WHAT WAS THE QUESTION?

Most people have more important things to do than to worry about what a city is or is supposed to be. They know all about cities anyway, because they were born in one, or because at one point in their life work, travel, love, or maybe even the promise of a better life brought them to the one they now live in. They know exactly what their city does and does not have to offer – either from experience, from talking to friends, or because their digital assistant recommended something to them. They know the route to work like the back of their hand, just like the stores around them, or how long you need to wait for which services. And, of course, they know where to find entertainment or distraction. More recently, people have got to know their cities in pandemic standstill.

One thing is clear, though: Some people love their city, others hate it, and most people don't spend much time thinking about the world, as long as it works.

That has probably been true since the birth of cities. What is *new* is the scale of things. At no other time have there been so many cities and never before have they been so large. Today, more than half of all human beings on earth live in a city, and there is no end in sight to urban growth. *New*, too, is the rise in cities' status, as well as the wealth of their problems and the sums that are spent on urban programmes. Never has self-improvement been at such a premium and has competition been fiercer. Finally, the scope for failure is also *new*, the threats posed by war, terrorism, and illnesses, as well as by radically changing economies, resource consumption, and man-made environmental change, in particular climate change.

All these factors force us to give the city more than a passing look. But how? As critical as the current problems are, the past can give us the decisive methodological nod. In his study of the origins of the city in the *Orient*, archaeologist *Hans J. Nissen* came to the conclusion that developments there could be understood as "the result of a series of specific responses to specific local challenges".[1] This realization contains a key idea. If the city is the answer, then what was the question? In other words: For which problem is the city a solution?

That is the guiding question of this book. I propose that the city can be understood as a tool – an old, incredibly versatile, and enduring tool for improving personal and collective opportunities. Tools can be used in very different ways. Shovels, for instance, can be used to dig the foundation for a house. But they have also on occasion been used to take people's lives. A detailed knowledge of a tool's characteristics can help us to understand both how to use it and, more importantly, what it *cannot* do.

---

1 Nissen, Hans J. (2005), Vom Weiler zur Großstadt im frühen Vorderen Orient, in: Falk, Harry (ed.) (2005), Wege zur Stadt. Entwicklung und Formen urbanen Lebens in der alten Welt. Bremen, p. 57.

If we consider the city to be a tool, it is astonishing how many people use it and how little we know about it. That is why this book attempts what is perhaps the hardest thing of all in a world that, as the Israeli historian *Yuval Noah Harari* among others has noted, is inundated with irrelevant information, namely clarity. And clarity, in a time of excess, is nothing other than power. This book seeks to shed light on humanity's most important tool.

To answer the question of what makes a city, this book aims to give the most concise answer possible. First, it explains why the city is such an important tool. This is followed by an examination of the approaches adopted by key "academic disciplines". We find that some texts are cited again and again. Therefore, in a kind of academic speed dating, we take a closer look at the ideas proposed and lessons learned by key experts. These two steps are necessary, but neither delivers convincing results. To delve deeper, the book applies a method proposed by the economist and sociologist *Werner Sombart*. Trusting in the intelligence of language, the word "*city*" and its semantic content is examined in a dozen of the world's languages. In doing so, following a concept drawn from the *philosophy of language*, we reveal something that we can call the "genes" of the city.

That, at least, is the theory. In practice, this method allows us to examine the still innumerable terms for and concepts and types of cities and to gain more clarity about what they mean. This is rounded off by an overview of some important issues that cities have to tackle today. And, in conclusion, we look to the future, which we at least know will be decided in and with the city, whether we are interested in it or not.

All of these rational ideas create a scientific overview – which is the least we can expect from academics. So as not to lose sight of the vibrancy and sensuality of urban life, these analyses are complemented by a few hopefully inspiring digressions.

Berlin, autumn 2020

NOTE ON THE ENGLISH EDITION

This book is the distilled essence of an exploratory journey that began back in the 1980s. Empirical-analytical case studies on the German city of Berlin during the Cold War were followed, in the early 1990s, by a city lexicon and, in 2005, by a comprehensive scholarly biography of the German capital. That study attempted a new, holistic "thick description" of the city that was inspired by the American anthropologist Clifford Geertz. Based on this "case", the following decade was spent formulating an interdisciplinary theory of the city. My book, published in German in 2020 under the title *Die Stadt*, summarizes the theoretical insights gained up to that point and outlines first practical applications.

The English edition of this book differs only in one respect from the German original in that I have deleted one infobox with literature tips in the section "City and countryside", as it refers solely to the German debate and is difficult to transfer to other languages and cultures. Other than that, the bibliographical references have been pared down somewhat by eliminating those titles that I presume are of only limited interest to an international readership. All referenced websites were checked when preparing this edition and, where available, were replaced by English sites.

Berlin, summer 2022

Table of contents

THE CITY IS THE ANSWER. BUT WHAT WAS THE QUESTION? 5

NOTE ON THE ENGLISH EDITION 7

I. THE DIFFICULTIES OF INTERDISCIPLINARITY 11

II. ON THE BENEFITS OF A TOOL 13

III. THEORY 17

A. The science of the city 17
1. The big picture (urbanism) 18
2. City as society (sociology and urban sociology) 19
3. City as market (economics and urban economics) 23
4. City as natural environment ((urban) geography, urban environmental management, and climate research) 24
5. City as design space (spatial planning, urban planning, architecture, and urban morphology) 26
6. City as policy (law) 28
7. City as memory space (history) 30
8. City as hope and disappointment (philosophy) 32
9. Ways out of no man's land (political science) 34
10. The city: a puzzle 36

B. The grand narratives 43
1. The good city (Aristotle) 43
2. The multifunctional city (Werner Sombart) 44
3. Politics, the market, and city types (Max Weber) 45
4. The blasé city dweller (Georg Simmel) 46
5. The dense city (Lewis Wirth and the Chicago School) 47
6. No city (Jürgen Friedrichs) 49
7. The global city (Saskia Sassen) 50
8. The ordinary city (Ash Amin and Stephen Graham) 52
9. The open city (Richard Sennett) 56
10. The experts' insights 57

C. The wisdom of languages: the city is 59
1. The city is dense infrastructure (Egyptian) 61
2. The city is citizenship (Greek) 61
3. The city is power politics (Latin) 63

4.	The city is structured densification (Spanish)	65
5.	The city is lifestyle (French)	66
6.	The city is relevance (English)	67
7.	The city is rights (German)	68
8.	The city is the centre (Russian)	70
9.	The city is civilization (Arabic)	70
10.	The city is prosperity (Hindi)	71
11.	The city is the economy (Chinese)	72
12.	The city is a hub (Japanese)	74
13.	The genes of the city	75

IV.	**PRACTICE**	**79**
A.	**Zooming in**	**79**
B.	**Terms, concepts, and city types**	**81**
1.	Megacity	82
2.	Global city	86
3.	Capital city	88
4.	Arrival city	94
5.	Smart city	96
6.	Neoliberal city	101
7.	Virus city	104
8.	Shrinking city and lost city	107
9.	Terms, concepts, and city types: valuable patterns?	110
C.	**Urban issues**	**116**
1.	Immigration and emigration	116
2.	Housing and living	118
3.	Society and the economy	120
4.	Movement and standstill	121
5.	Analogue and digital	123
6.	City and countryside	124
7.	City and world	125
8.	City and environment	128
9.	Diversity and reciprocities	129

V.	**OUR FUTURE WILL BE DECIDED IN AND WITH THE CITY**	**131**
	Literature	**135**
	Index	**138**

I. THE DIFFICULTIES OF INTERDISCIPLINARITY

The city lies crosswise. It is in all senses of the word too big to be an object of scientific investigation – too complex, too unwieldy for easy answers. That is why many academics conclude that holistic answers will not do. But that is not the only explanation for the lack of progress when it comes to research on the city. Its development has been horizontal, not vertical, and so there has been little advancement despite minor innovations, and an overview is at best available for individual disciplines. Following well-travelled paths is, therefore, insufficient to get a handle on the city.

This introduction attempts to break new ground. It should be seen as an experiment. It began with an incident and an encounter with one of the greatest contradictions in contemporary social sciences.

The incident occurred during a working day at a trade fair in *Shanghai* gone wrong. It was late, and my colleagues had all long since gone back to their hotels. In front of the trade centre, I found that public transportation had shut down for the day and there were no more taxis to be had. As it was long past midnight, the only way back to my bed, around 10 kilometres away, was on foot. Even back then, Shanghai was already one of the second-tier global cities. Recalling *Saskia Sassen's* eponymous study, which I had read not that long before, I walked past multiple *residential cities*, at least two *industrial cities*, a pristine *smart city*, an *old city*, and, finally, in *Pudong*, a *global city*. What was Shanghai then? I asked myself. One of those city types? A global city? Or all of them together? These thoughts prompted me to ask the fundamental question: What is a city?

Each of the above-mentioned prototypical city types can be adequately described, but it is not clear how they are connected. There were no criteria for making an informed assessment.

My search for an answer led me to those disciplines that have examined urban life, which revealed a contradiction. On the one hand, everyone is agreed that the city is complex and can only be grasped via an interdisciplinary approach. Research on the city even gave birth to a new discipline that is meant to provide an overview: *urban studies*.

But after theory comes practice. Interdisciplinarity is an admirable goal, but science is divided into disciplines and that is how research is in the main conducted. Hence all researchers of the city are confronted with the dilemma of the necessity of interdisciplinary investigation without being able to cope with the scope of this task. Furthermore, experts fear the criticism of colleagues from other disciplines if they spend too much time butting in where they do not belong.

Pragmatism reigns. While answering the key questions nearly always means having to think outside the box, anyone who takes the risk of doing so is usually timid about proposing their solutions. Few researchers have made serious inroads into interdisciplinarity. One exception in the field at hand is *Saskia Sassen*, whose highly innovative "Global Cities" study links *sociology* and economics, although the latter discipline has been happy to ignore her to this day. Or the geographer *Elisabeth Lichtenberger*, whose best works connect *geography, history, urban planning, sociology*, and *economics*, with illuminating results.

Interdisciplinarity is no small risk, but it is often rewarded with insights that could not have otherwise been gained. Along its arduous path lie questions that must be answered, such as: "Why should geographers be interested in the etymology of the word 'city' in 12 languages?" Yet the answer is obvious: Because knowing it makes them smarter and increases the value of their expertise, transforming it from an individual well-crafted tile into part of a mosaic. Through interdisciplinarity it may be possible to eradicate one of the greatest weaknesses of urban studies, namely that the relationship between individual insights is rarely explained. As a result, we know the price of everything, but rarely the value.

Any interdisciplinary approach raises the question of who is applying it. My doctoral studies were in political science and my post-doctoral thesis was in the field of history. Since the 1980s, I have been interested in the city as a research area, at first in an empirical analysis of the role of Berlin during the Cold War. That was followed by the creation of an encyclopaedia of the city of Berlin, commissioned by the Berlin Senate, as well as academic essays on the city and the description and theories of the city.

Looking at the city from an interdisciplinary perspective entails delving into a variety of disciplines. The most important tools for gaining such an overview are handbooks, encyclopaedias, and surveys. Going through this wealth of resources takes time – in this case around 10 years. Ignoring the maxim "publish or perish", however, has often been rewarded with surprising results.

This introduction is, therefore, an attempt to learn from other disciplines. What has been most fruitful is not only the answers provided by individual disciplines, but even more so their way of asking questions. They radically changed my idea of the city. And so, in the hope that this study can do the same for other inquiring minds, let us begin.

II. ON THE BENEFITS OF A TOOL

We do not know who built the first city. We do not know where it was erected or when, or by whom, and certainly not why. But we do at least have evidence enough to make an educated guess. While the exact site of the first city is not known, we can be fairly certain of the general area: the *Fertile Crescent*, as the American Egyptologist and historian *James Henry Breasted* called the winter rain area north of the Syrian desert in 1916.[2]

Figure 1. The Fertile Crescent extends from southeast to southwest along the northern bank of the Persian Gulf, including parts of what are now Iraq, Syria, Lebanon, Israel, Palestine, and Jordan. Occasionally northern Egypt is also included in the area.

Many of the ruins of ancient cities found to date are situated in this area. Whether or not one of these sites was in fact the first or oldest city is a question of the definition used. When does a settlement become a city? When is it large enough? When it has a certain number of inhabitants or when it covers a certain area? When a particular population density has been reached? When it has large buildings? When there is evidence of a division of labour, diversity of population, or even of transregional functions?

Depending on one's viewpoint, there are many candidates for the title of the first city.

---

2 Hans J. Nissen provides an up-to-date, scientifically precise overview in his history of the ancient central Asian region, in which he also explores the geographical and climatic conditions that made a sedentary lifestyle possible. See Nissen, Hans J. (2012), Geschichte Altvorderasiens. Munich, p. 6–11 and p. 23–9.

Çatalhöyük is a favourite. A large settlement with many thousands of permanent residents, it was situated on the Anatolian Plateau in what is now Turkey. In terms of *size* and *density*, Çatalhöyük fulfils two of the defining criteria of a city. Yet nothing has yet been found to show that it met other criteria, for example that it functioned as a *hub*. However, only around 5 per cent of the hill has been excavated, so it is too early to make a final assessment. We do know how old Çatalhöyük is: Its oldest parts date to ca. 7500 BCE, that is they are around 9,500 years old.

The site exhibits two features that speak against defining it as a city as we usually understand the term. It has neither streets nor squares; the houses abut each other and were perhaps accessed via ladders from the roofs. And its development contradicts most accepted theories of cities,[3] according to which smaller settlements grow gradually. Çatalhöyük seems to have been planned as a large settlement from its inception – a riddle that has yet to be solved.

Another candidate is *Jericho*, in what are now the Autonomous Palestinian Territories on the west bank of the River Jordan. The city claims to be the oldest city in the world, based on the remnants of towers and walls. However, these are not former city walls, as was first assumed, but a local feature. It is fairly certain that the settlement has been continuously inhabited since the 10th century BCE. But it is unclear whether this old settlement can be called a city.

A third candidate for the title of the oldest city lies outside of the Fertile Crescent. Discovered by Indian divers in 2002, it was given the prosaic name "GKCC", *Gulf of Khambhat Cultural Complex*. It is quite a large settlement located at a depth of around 20 to 40 metres in the Gulf of Cambay in the Arabian Sea, in Gujarat State, India. Excavations have only recently begun. One of the artifacts found, a piece of wood, has been dated twice, once at 7190 BCE and once at 7545 to 7490 BCE. Yet from the evidence to date, it is a disputed matter whether it can be called a city or even a civilization.

Çatalhöyük, *Jericho*, and *GKCC* are not cities. At best, all three are early forms of large settlements. It is also still unclear which questions they answer. What is certain, though, is that these answers were not permanent, for all these finds have been singular and nothing points to any of these sites having become a catalyst for long-term settlements. Their models do not seem to have been copied.

---

3   de.wikipedia.org/wiki/Stadtentstehung (accessed: 23 Apr. 2022). A fundamental text on function as a key aspect: Christaller, Walter (1968, original 1933), Die zentralen Orte in Süddeutschland. Darmstadt.

Figures 2–4. Çatalhöyük in Anatolia, reconstruction by the Museum of Pre- and Ancient History, Weimar | Jericho | Gulf of Khambhat Cultural Complex (GKCC) on the Indian coast.

On the contrary, no remains of large settlements have yet been found that can be dated to the following 3,000 years. From that time on, however, there seems to have been some advantage to living close together in larger settlements. Many sites, including *Eridu*, *Ur*, *Tell Brak*, and *Byblos*, all within the Fertile Crescent, have been dated between 5000 and 4000 BCE. Since then, the city has always been a form of human settlement.

We can thus draw two initial conclusions: For one, we know the area in which the city first developed, even if we do not know the exact site. It was the Fertile Crescent, or more exactly the Near East and (to include the *Gulf of Khambat Cultural Complex*) nearby regions. All of the large settlements found in other areas to date, whether in *China* or the *Americas*, were erected much later.

We also know around when the first cities appeared. If we regard the oldest finds as preliminary forms, we can safely say that since the 5th century BCE at the latest, or around 7,000 to 6,000 years ago, many people made the decision to live together in a form of settlement that we today call a city.

To which question is the city of that period the answer? Researchers' findings suggest that from that time on, this special form of living together provided long-term advantages, created new opportunities, and was flexible enough to adapt to new conditions. This verdict has stood the test of time. Seen this way, the city is not only a collection of buildings and people, it is more than anything an instrument and a method – a *tool*.

That is why those analyses fall short that claim that the *cities of antiquity* cannot be compared to modern *industrial cities* or to *smart cities*. On the one hand, this statement is a banality. Of course, cultural practices and technologies shape the form of the city in every era. On the other hand, this statement is simply false. For example, given a city like *Pompeii*, buried in the Vesuvius eruption of 79 CE and excavated in the modern era, we could easily fill it with urban life within hours, including infrastructure – from street food to Wi-Fi.

It is, therefore, important to decode the features and character of this tool that humans have been using for 200 to 250 generations across the globe, shaping our planet. The city is without a doubt one of the most astonishing inventions in the history of humankind. Even the examples named above exhibit features that are still found in today's urban centres. Let us thus try to decode these features, in a first step by turning to the relevant academic disciplines and their answers to the question: What is a city?

III. THEORY

A. The science of the city

If something needs to be calculated, we turn to mathematics, when there is a structure to build, engineering provides the answers, and medicine knows best in case of illness. But who is responsible for cities? The rather unhelpful answer is: everyone and no one. Cities are so complex that one discipline can at best focus on one particular aspect. More than a dozen disciplines contribute to our understanding, and the overview in *Table 1* is far from complete.

Table 1. Disciplines involved in urban research

1)	Urbanism	Interdisciplinary, greatest promise for urban research
2)	Sociology	Closely related, but not identical; have made substantial contributions to research; currently the leading discipline
3)	Urban sociology	
4)	Economics	Currently doing little research on cities, but offer a wealth of historical knowledge; (urban) sociologists often draw on economic findings for their theories
5)	Urban economics	
6)	Geography	Closely related but not identical; geography in particular is often wide in scope
7)	Urban geography	
8)	Urban ecology	
9–10)	Spatial and urban planning	Dominate practical work, but engage in little theoretical work
11)	Architecture	
12)	Urban morphology	
13)	Law	Also examines the city where appropriate; large body of historical knowledge
14)	History	Examines, in particular, kingdoms, dynasties, epochs, events, people etc.; source of many histories and biographies of cities; theoretical or methodological research is rare
15)	Archaeology	Main source of knowledge about the origins of cities
16)	Classical studies	Source of important methodological foundations
17)	National/regional history	Individual focus and traditional methodology; sometimes innovative
18)	Philosophy	Offers a normative perspective on cities
19)	Political science	Concentration on municipal politics; does not, for example, take into consideration that cities are also global players; urban politics perhaps promises a new approach
20)	Urban politics	
21)	Social science	Umbrella term that gathers results in overviews, encyclopaedias, and anthologies

NB: Some subdisciplines work with different terminology.

Despite their differences, all the academic fields agree that it is only possible to understand the city using an interdisciplinary approach. Yet despite this consensus, it has proven almost impossible to put interdisciplinary research into practice. Who would dare claim to have an overview of more than 20 disciplines? For an initial exploration of the subject, it is therefore most useful to look at the encyclopaedias and introductory volumes that the individual disciplines have produced.

1. The big picture (urbanism)

Urbanism perhaps offers the greatest promise for research on the city. It is the only field that is decidedly interdisciplinary in focus and – not to be underestimated – works with one of the strongest concepts, that is *"urbanitas"*. The Latin term originally designated a style that was perspicacious, elegant, and witty. This connotation still exists in the many fashion labels, furniture designers, real estate portals etc. that have "urban" in their company name. The use of the concept in modern science dates back to the Catalonian city planner *Ildefons Cerdà*. After the city walls of *Barcelona* were torn down, he sought a new approach to city planning and, finding no reference work, wrote one himself. His *General Theory of Urbanization*, published in 1867, was concerned with designing cities to promote social life.[4] That was his recipe for contemporary urbanity. Cerdà's was the first work in which the term appeared in modernity. To this day, the term is usually used sociologically and descriptively or normatively and aesthetically.

It is easy to trace the various debates as urbanism has evolved as a subject. In research done in the 1970s, to name just one example, the term "planning" was ubiquitous, today it is rarely used. Contemporary debates are less prone to generalizations; their scope is broader, and they are more willing to reflect on newer methods.

At the same time, the term "urbanism" is used programmatically, for example to draw together urban management demands (*"new urbanism"*) or, since the late 1980s, as a backlash against *"urban sprawl"*.

Because the terminology is so broad, it can be interpreted in many ways. That is its strength – and its weakness. There is no clear analytical definition of urbanism. Nevertheless, there is consensus that urbanism integrates varying disciplines and approaches, without being an umbrella term. "Urbanism", as one of the key books on the subject contests, "like no comparable term, comprises both a fundamentally interdisciplinary perspective and brings together all the various levels involved in urban development: analysis, planning and design, steering, and critical reflection on what has been achieved".[5] "Nothing," writes the sociologist *Peter Noller*, "is united under this term. For that one would need

---

4 Sennett, Richard (2018), Building and Dwelling. Ethics for the City. New York, p. 37.
5 All citations on this page are taken from: Frey, Oliver; Koch, Florian (eds.) (2011), II. Gesellschaft, Governance, Gestaltung, Vienna, Berlin. More specifically: Tilman Harlander, p. 17; Peter Noller, p. 15–16; Sibylla Zech, p. 14; Klaus R. Kunzmann, p. 19.

a concrete question, a programme, or a scientific concept. … Urbanism holds together that which constitutes urbanity". And, in fact, urbanism has yet to develop its own method or even theory. Structural thinking predominates, built on traditional hierarchical models as in other disciplines. This concept is one of the greatest problems in urban research. It divides the world into levels, distinguishing between *global, international, national, regional,* and *local*. The city forms the final level. This view has serious flaws, for it fails to convincingly take our globalized present into account and can hardly explain phenomena such as the *global city*. This is not the only example in which basic concepts in the field are underdefined.

📖 Frey, Oliver; Koch, Florian (eds.) (2011a), Positionen zur Urbanistik I. Stadtkultur und neue Methoden der Stadtforschung. Vienna, Berlin.

Frey, Oliver; Koch, Florian (eds.) (2011b), Positionen zur Urbanistik II: Gesellschaft, Governance, Gestaltung. Vienna, Berlin.

The best anthologies that I know of on the current state of research.

What does urbanism add to our understanding of the city? It has strong terms and its aspirations are big enough to do the city justice. However, it has yet to develop a clear profile. For the time being it is a promise that is connected to the hope that "it will be better able to prevail as an academic discipline within the next one hundred years". As yet, the discipline does not have the prerogative of interpretation when it comes to the issue – that is the purview of sociology and urban sociology.

2. City as society (sociology and urban sociology)

No other discipline has looked so extensively and so intensively at the city as sociology. The discipline's founders, *Max Weber*, *Ferdinand Tönnies*, and *Georg Simmel*, contributed influential ideas, some of which we will look at more closely in the next chapter.[6] Many works from the early days of sociology remain notable today, especially those out of the *Chicago School*, the most influential school on interpreting urban life.

Important members of the Chicago School include *Robert Ezra Park*, *Ernes Burgess*, and *Lewis Wirth*. Inspired by Weber and Simmel, under whom he had studied in Berlin in 1899–90, Park founded the *Department of Sociology* at the *University of Chicago* in the 1920s that went on to become the home of seminal works in microsociology and minority and poverty studies. The school produced a canon of urban research that was wedded to reality, had a sense of mission, and a desire to reach a broad public. At the same time, its works exhibited a "dis-

---

6 Tönnies, Ferdinand (1887), Community and Civil Society, trans. by Jose Harris and Margaret Hollis. Cambridge, p. 26–27. Simmel, Georg (1984, original 1903), The Metropolis and Mental Life, in: Simmel, Georg (1984), On Individuality and Social Forms. Chicago, p. 324–339. Weber, May (1958, original 1922), The City, trans. by Gertrud Neuwirth. Glencoe.

connection from and indifference to the physical city".[7] For the Chicago School, the city was a social experiment or laboratory. And, in truth, the vitality of the work that came out of it should not distract from the fact that its perspective is very mechanical and formal. It aims at *social engineering*, and urban planning is its tool.

Thus, the *Chicago School* can be seen as a counterpart to another key position, epitomized by *Jane Jacobs*'s book *The Death and Life of Great American Cities*. Jacobs called for the city to be seen as more than just a functional system, advocating, as *Richard Sennett* wrote, "for mixed neighbourhoods, for informal street life and for local control" in lieu of large-scale master plans.

This created two opposing positions: for one thing, there is Jacobs's rejection of the large-scale designs of *Ildefons Cerdà (Barcelona), Georges-Eugène Baron Haussmann (Paris)*, or even *Frederick Law Olmstedt (New York)* or the influential *Athens Charter*. Second, she thus attacks one of the other leading leftist urban researchers, that is *Lewis Mumford*. Mumford was sceptical of Jacobs's position and countered "in the name of socialism", as Sennett relates, "that to fight capitalist top-down power, you need a sweeping countervailing force". It is already clear that sociological positions are intertwined with city planning and architecture.

Of sociology and urban sociology it can be said that the work of the first two generations in particular remain benchmarks when it comes to the state of research. Building on them, three lines of research gained traction in the second half of the 20th century:[8]

1) From the 1960s and 1970s, leftist research increasingly developed (spatial) sociological theories that were given significant impetus through the works of *Henri Lefebvre*. A direct line can be drawn from there to *Manuel Castells*'s *Space of Flows*. These researchers interpreted the city as a social space, with the aim of righting the flaws they found – for example unequal opportunities – by restructuring or redistributing space. *Dieter Hoffmann-Axthelm*, a radical protagonist of this faction, propagates a fundamental reassessment and redistribution of urban space, and in the end a recreation of the city.
2) A second line of development took place in the area of post-war urban planning and, from the 1990s, the political and spatial realignment of Central Europe. The subdiscipline urban sociology grew out of this discussion. The work of *Hartmut Häußermann* is exemplary for this faction, as its covers the entire spectrum of this topic.
3) But the undoubtedly most important development was in relation to *globalization*, and increasingly also the *digital transformation* within and through

---

7   Sennett, Richard (2018), p. 69. A further quotation at the end of the next paragraph: ibid, p. 78.
8   Castells, Manuel (1996–1998), The Information Age: Economy, Society, and Culture. Oxford, Malden MA. Vol. 1 (1996), The Rise of the Network Society | Vol. 2 (1997), The Power of Identity | Vol. 3 (1998), End of Millennium. See also Sassen, Saskia (1991), The Global City. New York, London, Tokyo.

cities. What was key in this debate was *Saskia Sassen*'s seminal work *The Global City*. Sassen recognized this type of city as the main driver of globalization. Her thesis amounted to no less than a completely new assessment of the role of the city in *international relations*. The importance of her ideas and the paradigm shift she initiated is only gradually becoming clear.

The first and third positions in particular point towards a core problem of urban sociological research: the delineation of "city" and "society". *Society* is perhaps the most important category in sociology. Its roots reach back to Aristotle's view of people as *zóon politikón*, creatures whose nature it is to live in society. The term became popular during the Enlightenment, and the emerging middle class used it to underline their self-understanding as a "citizen" society – as opposed to, for example, a feudal state.

The concept of society has always been connected to ideas of space, and the *state* became the main conceptual figure in modernity. Society is a hierarchical concept, it is the main category under which institutions such as state, family, law, or education form subcategories. The city can also be placed within this hierarchy, and as long as the boundaries are clear, this model makes sense. This is particularly true for the 19th and 20th centuries, a phase in which states were strong and there was no need to draw a distinction between the state and society. Today, however, other phenomena have taken centre stage, such as global financial flows, the digital transformation, or new forms of living together. These cannot be clearly delineated using traditional terminology. While categories such as family, state, and society still hold meaning, their content is shifting and they are insufficient when it comes to explaining contemporary forms of living. Just as the city can no longer be seen as a subcategory of the state, neither can it be regarded as a subcategory of society.

This problem is exacerbated by the fact that many authors see the city mostly as the *stage* on which societal conflicts play out. For them, there is no need to draw a distinction between "social society" and "urban society". The most radical proponent of this viewpoint is the sociologist *Jürgen Friedrichs*, whom we will look at briefly in III.B.6. He is vehemently against any such division.[9] And so placing the city in context remains a major challenge of sociological urban research. There is, currently, no one prevailing opinion. Recent work on the *sociology of space* aims at providing an understanding of the delimitation and dynamization of space. It thus has similarities with the concept of *governance* in political science that seeks to expand the boundaries of the classic definition of politics and to establish a new understanding. Other authors propose speaking only of a lower or higher density of spatial structures.

---

9   Friedrichs, Jürgen (1997), Stadtanalyse. Soziale und räumliche Organisation der Gesellschaft. Reinbek.

> Besides the classics by Max Weber, Werner Sombart, and Georg Simmel discussed in detail in II.B.:
>
> Tönnies, Ferdinand (2001, original 1887), Community and Civil Society, trans. by Jose Harris and Margaret Hollis. Cambridge. (Subtitle in the German: A Treatise on Communism and Socialism as Empirical Forms of Culture).
>
> Mumford, Lewis (1961), The City in History. Its Origins, Its Transformations, and Its Prospects. Boston. *Grand progressive overview.*
>
> Jacobs, Jane (1961), The Death and Life of Great American Cities. New York. *A response to Mumford.*
>
> *Still one of the best answers to the question of what a society is:* Heinrich Popitz, (2011) Allgemeine Soziologische Theorie. Konstanz. *A collection of Popitz's 1966 lectures on sociological theory. Lectures I–VI, p. 15–90, are particularly interesting.*

At such an abstract level, it is impossible to contradict one or other position. Nevertheless, the conclusion remains unsatisfactory. Reducing city, state, and society to spatial structures that need only be described and calculated is unconvincing. Taken to the extreme, it would mean that the city is no more than a form in which humans live mostly dependent on spatial structures – a very one-dimensional view of people and their world.

This harks back to an old debate that goes well beyond sociology and into the fields of ethnology and philosophy. It is controversial whether structures or conditions influence human beings or vice versa. There is no meaningful way to answer such a generalized question. Since the influences are reciprocal, satisfying answers can only be given in concrete cases.

The complexity of the questions reveal the very broad scope and diversity of sociological approaches. It also reveals the many small but important differences within and between sociology and urban sociology. As close as they are, there are many key differences when one looks in detail at their understanding. For that reason, this discipline has not yet delivered a generally accepted analytical definition of the city. Instead, there are many often similar, and sometimes completely contradictory, definitions, as can be seen in the many encyclopaedias and handbooks. While contributions to encyclopaedia often list only a few key characteristics of cities, the number of features grew after urban sociology was established. Yet these criteria are almost never drawn together to form a definition. If there is consensus at all, it is that the terms *size*, *density*, and *diversity* are necessary but insufficient to any description of the city. Thus while none of the varying branches of sociology define the city, they have given us many well-founded contributions towards an understanding of the city.

One more thing should be noted: From the founders of the discipline to the present, sociologists have always made an effort to look beyond their own discipline. One of their greatest interests has always been in economics, a feeling that has so far not really been reciprocated.

3. City as market (economics and urban economics)

The city is not the main focus of contemporary economics. Comprehensive explorations are exceptions, and discussions of the city, if they take place at all, are brief. A good example is the largest German encyclopaedia of economics, the *Gabler Wirtschaftslexikon,* which devotes all of three sentences to the city. However, these sentences are worth looking at more closely. In essence, the city is "in contrast to the country or rural areas, a large, dense settlement with specific functions of the spatial division of labour and political rule, depending upon the societal organization and form of production".[10]

Despite its brevity, the text names five characteristics of the city: 1) its being in contrast to rural areas, 2) size and densification, 3) spatial division of labour, 4) political rule, and 5) its dependence on the form of society and form of production. This understanding points out an important link. When division of labour and political rule are dependent on the form of production and of society, then the latter are fundamental. That is a clear prioritization. This definition is in the tradition of *Max Weber,* who saw the city predominantly as an economic structure in its function as a market. Strangely, the text references neither the market nor Weber.

Overall, economic analyses rarely draw from other disciplines in their discussion of the city. This is despite the fact that many economic subdisciplines deal with issues that go beyond pure economics, for example political economics, which has often discussed the relationship between the state and the economy. Since the 1980s, the dominant trend in economics has been *neoliberalism* and, concurrently, privatization, which has had two key impacts on the city.

1) For one, in the course of *globalization* the city has become a global player. Yet economic discussions of the subject reveal a strange blind spot. While globalization is dealt with often and exhaustively, the corresponding urban model is hardly ever mentioned in economic surveys, not even as an example.
2) What is also important in this discussion is *municipal management,* once an influential and extensively researched subdiscipline that is now widely ignored. In the 19th and 20th centuries, this field in many European cities developed into a key economic sector with powerful municipal services. For the emerging middle classes, it offered a chance to secure a place in a society that was still influenced by courtly structures.

In the last three decades of the 20th century, urban centres reduced these activities or gave them up entirely. Budget deficits, the need to save costs, and the desire for more efficiency were the main drivers behind these developments. While some problems were solved, new dependencies were created, especially on private service providers, which in turn limited the ability of municipal

---

10 Gablers Wirtschaftslexikon (2004), Wiesbaden. Vol. 1, p. 2765–2785, Vol. 2, p. 1701–1705.

authorities to manage urban areas via policy. This development is now widely criticized and has in some cases been partially revised.

Currently, urban economics is gaining ground again and concentrates in the main on 1) the development of urban areas, 2) the analysis of developmental patterns in urban areas, 3) the spatial dimension of urban problems, 4) the spatial dimensions of local politics, and 5) the relationship between the city and its periphery.

What, then, do economics and urban economics contribute to our understanding of the city? Currently, it must be said, economics has the potential to offer more. Especially since the discipline will have to deal with an important issue going forward: In light of the growth of the world population from 2.53 billion in 1950 to almost 8 billion today, and the concurrently growing need for resources and environmental impacts, it is clear that the liberal understanding of the market and its orientation towards growth, now held by the third generation of economists, does not have much of a future. Technological innovations alone will not solve these problems. Since urban areas play a key role in any process of reorientation, an increased interest in urban economics is on the cards. The global pandemic that began in China in 2019 and its global economic impact is likely to accelerate this shift in thinking. Taking the spatial orientation of urban economics as our anchor, our focus shifts to the urban space itself. That leads us to those disciplines that have this as their research focus.

📖 Glaeser, Edwards (2011), Triumph of the City. How urban spaces make us human. London. *The foremost expert's best book.*

O'Sullivan, Arthur (2011), Urban Economics. New York. *An introduction with an international perspective.*

Mills, Edwin; Hamilton, Bruce W. (1994), Urban Economics. New Jersey. *Pioneering work on regional economics.*

4. City as natural environment ((urban) geography, urban environmental management, and climate research)

(Urban) geography

Both geography and urban geography are among the more innovative disciplines in terms of their approach to the city. In recent years, their scholars have produced substantial works on the topic. Yet their understanding of the subject does exhibit some peculiar features, as the following example illustrates. The *Lexikon der Geographie*, one of the discipline's standard encyclopaedias, defines the city as an "administrative unit under municipal law with a certain population, population density, and occupational structure".[11] These characteristics, dutifully named in almost all geographical works, are as unexciting as they are unspecific to the discipline. To show that they have understood this – a ritual

---

11   Brunotte, Ernst; Gebhardt, Hans; Meurer, Manfred; Meusburger, Peter; Nipper, Josef (eds.) (2002), Lexikon der Geographie in 4 Bänden. Heidelberg, Berlin. Vol. 2, p. 262.

repeated in all disciplines – scholars often combine such statements with a rejection of any holistic concept of the city.

That would be unremarkable if they then went on to study the object itself after having expressed this caveat. Instead, geographers have developed a great passion for ignoring this warning the moment they issue it and defining the city anyway – for their own purposes, of course. These definitions are more thorough and precise than in almost any other field. Geographers have, for example, identified not only a handful of characteristics of urban areas, but many more. They include 1) a large population, organized in groups or classes; 2) a relatively enclosed site with 3) densely built-up areas; 4) a concentration of workplaces that are 5) not agricultural; 6) multifunctionality; 7) a division of labour in the secondary and tertiary sectors; 8) a central infrastructure; 9) relevance as a transport hub; 10) a way of living that can be distinguished from rural lifestyles; and 11) internal differentiation; in particular 12) the creation of neighbourhoods. But while these disciplines have isolated these characteristics so precisely, they have as yet been unable to consolidate them.

Still, it must be said that these features do provide a fairly exact description of the city. This diligence can be seen as the result of historical experience. Post-war works in particular can be understood as answers to arguments put forward in the 19th and early 20th centuries that often leant themselves to misuse. One example is *Friedrich Ratzel*'s influential book *Anthropogeographie*.[12] Ratzel broke new ground with his concept of "political geography", which drew on *Charles Darwin*'s theory of evolution, yet his idea of *Lebensraum* was perverted by the Nazis to support their murderous ideology.

As a result, scholars in the discipline are meticulous about reflecting on the field's central concepts. In light of this precision, it is no wonder that this discipline has produced *the* milestone of urban research, the eight-volume *Handbook of Urban Studies*, that brings together 146 essays by the top researchers in the field, including essential classic works by *Max Weber*, *Lewis Mumford*, *Louis Wirth*, and *Fernand Braudel*.

> *The literature in these fields is notable for its meticulousness, its precise argumentation, and its original approaches. Of all the disciplines, geography thinks the furthest outside its own box. The handbooks come highly recommended.*
>
> Lichtenberger, Elisabeth (2002), Die Stadt. Von der Polis zur Metropolis. Darmstadt. *An overview by one of Germany's most renowned geographers and one of the few researchers whose work is interdisciplinary.*
>
> Outstanding: Paddison, Ronan (ed.) (2001), Handbook of Urban Studies. London; Paddison, Ronan; Timberlake, Michael (eds.) (2009), Urban Studies: Economy. Los Angeles. Vol. I: What are Cities? – Vol. II: The Urban Economy – Vol. III: Connected Cities – Hinterlands, Hierarchies, Networks and Beyond – Vol. IV: Political Economy of Real Estate – Social and Political Aspects of Urban Development.
>
> Paddison, Ronan; Ostendorf, Wim (eds.) (2009), Urban Studies. Society. Los Angeles. Vol. I: Cities as Social Spaces – Vol. II: Experience the City – Vol. III: Designing and Planning Cities – Vol. IV: Cities, Ideas and Ideals.

---

12 Ratzel, Friedrich (1975, original 1891), Anthropogeographie. Darmstadt, p. 464–509.

Urban ecology

Urban ecology is a comparatively young discipline, although its roots go back to the 18th century. One of the first people to engage with the subject was the English botanist *Thomas Fairchild*. His 1722 book, *The City Gardener,* was the first to call attention to the recreational function of parks and gardens and to the negative impact of air pollution.

Current research in the field, which investigates the interaction between urban areas and the natural environment, mainly focuses on 1) the application of environmental questions and methods to urban habitats; 2) the analysis of cities as ecosystems, in particular a macro view of cities and their ecological footprint; and 3) the creation of ecological and sustainability criteria for urban development and planning, the aim being to have a "green" or "sustainable" city.

Climate research

The discipline of geography is closely connected to *climate research* and the important results it has produced in recent years. While there is consensus that humans have caused the climate to change considerably, it is hard to go beyond sweepingly general statements regarding what exactly those changes are and what their individual impacts are.[13] In the meantime, concrete prognoses can, however, be made for numerous cities. For example, at the beginning of the 20th century, summer temperatures in central Europe exceeded 25° Celsius (77° Fahrenheit) on around between 35 and 37 days a year. By the end of the century, that number had risen to between 89 and 92 days a year. This has far-reaching consequences for dense urban areas.

Geography, urban geography, urban ecology, and climate research offer highly relevant, precise, and informed answers to the question of what a city is. The methodological tools used to describe natural environments within cities are now very precise. The only significant gaps are found in ecology and climate research. While persuasive research results exist for both the local and the global level, the question of interdependencies and reciprocal impacts remains open. Closely related to the disciplines that study natural urban spaces are those that actively shape urban space.

5. City as design space (spatial planning, urban planning, architecture, and urban morphology)

These four disciplines are primarily practice-oriented. Urban planning and architecture are among the oldest fields that design cities. Their main focus is planning, structuring, and using space. Let us first look at *spatial planning*, which exhibits some interesting particularities in its view of the city. One is the key concept of *Raumbeanspruchung*, or how space is used. This idea, which

---

13 Rahmstorf, Stefan; Schellhuber, Hans Joachim (2006), Der Klimawandel. Munich.

stems from geography, delineates more than simply how much space is taken up. It sees the city as a spatial structure, which enables a better understanding of large cities in particular. Also central to this field is its focus on "weight" and "connectedness" in the use of space.

While *spatial planning* is interested in the description and management of space, *urban morphology* investigates the form of the city and the physical formation processes within the body of the settlement. The focus is on the division and management of city lots and how they are built up. City maps and plans and their analysis are its most important tools.

All four fields rarely formulate an understanding of the city. Scholars reflect a lot on what their field has done for the city, occasionally they also examine what mistakes have been made, and almost always they expound upon what the city could and should be. But they almost never define what "city" means to them.[14] Apparently they believe that it is so self-evident that no further elaboration is necessary. While that may be true of the fields as a whole, many individuals have made fundamental investigations of the city. Their ideas are often radical, sometimes polemical, and always interesting. Examples range from *Le Corbusier*'s 1925 publication *Urbanism* to *Rem Koolhaas*'s 1978 examination of Manhattan, *Delirious New York*. Architects have occasionally made an attempt at a fundamental definition of urban design, for example at the *Congrès Internationaux d'Architecture Moderne* (CIAM), which focused on urban management from 1928 to 1954. The influential *Athens Charter*, published

📖 *A complete overview of the literature is impossible. Three illuminating books:*

Sitte, Camillo (1944, original 1889), The Art of Building Cities: City Building According to its Artistic Fundamentals, trans. Charles Stewart. New York.

Heinrich, Klaus (2015), Dahlemer Vorlesungen – Karl Friedrich Schinkel/Albert Speer, Arch+ 219. *In this "Dahlem lecture" the religious philosopher examines the links between Classicism and National Socialist architecture. Fascinating and eye-opening.*

Posener, Julius (1972), From Schinkel to the Bauhaus. Five lectures on the growth of modern German architecture. London. *Magical.*

ⓘ *The Athens Charter*

A summary of the *IV Congrès Internationaux d'Architecture Moderne* in 1933, the Charter advocates for a functional city and the end of traditional urban development. Its aim was the functional separation of living units (in large housing projects), offices, shopping, trade, and industry. Large open areas connected by individual motor traffic (*car-friendly cities*) became one of its guiding principles. The disadvantages of this model have become clear since the 1970s, and its concept is now considered outdated.

---

14 The two-volume *Oxford Companion to Architecture* discusses architects, engineers, design aspects, building types, epochs, styles, and architecture in many different countries and contains definitions of concepts and information on materials, movements, services, and structures, but there are no texts devoted to the *city*, the *town*, or *urbanism*. The three-volume collection on urban planning edited by Vittorio Magnago Lampugnani et al. contains 167 texts. It explores architectonic thought from the Enlightenment to the present. But it does not contain a single text explaining what a city is. Goode, Patrick (ed.) (2009), Oxford Companion to Architecture. Oxford. Lampugnani, Vittorio Magnago; Frey, Katja; Perotti, Eliana (eds.) (2008), Anthologie zum Städtebau. Von der Stadt der Aufklärung zur Metropole des industriellen Zeitalters. Vol. I.1. and Vol. I.2. Berlin.

in 1933, on the urban design of the future is one of the best-known results of the CIAM.

To this day, none of the four disciplines has produced its own, spatially oriented and widely accepted concept of the city. Architectural works in particular are loathe to say what they mean by a city, almost always evading the question and instead offering up a grab-bag of possibilities. For architects, the city seems first and foremost to be an object of aesthetic, technical, and social engineering. This viewpoint is brought back down to earth by a discipline that is usually overlooked in discussions of the city, that is jurisprudence.

6. City as policy (law)

Since the *Babylonian* era, the law has been one of the most important instruments of conflict resolution. It deals with all areas of life, including many questions that are relevant in and to cities and are tried there. Yet the city itself is seldom an object of contemporary research and only occasionally plays a role in the discipline. In legalese, that sounds like this: "The delineation of a larger community as a c. by the Municipal Codes (*Gemeindeordnungen der Länder*) is of no legal import."[15] For those not versed in law, this means that the city is not an independent legal body in Germany, in contrast to the state or the federal states, or *Bundesländer*. Rather, a city is no more than "one of the many special names for a community".

📖 *On city charters:* Bader, Karl Siegfried; Dilcher, Gerhard (eds.) (1999), Deutsche Rechtsgeschichte. Land und Stadt – Bürger und Bauer im Alten Europa. Berlin.

One exception to this rule that is beyond the scope of this study are *town twinning programmes*. More important, however, (we shall see why at the end of this section) are historical cases, of which I shall briefly outline two: medieval city charters and *"Berlin (West)"* – written exactly so. In medieval times, it was said that "city air makes you free" because of a law that serfs became free after a year and a day in the city, which can be seen as a precursor to the rule of law. In the second case, the Allied powers' law of occupation and its implementation helped prevent the *Cold War* from heating up. These are two historical examples in which jurisprudence is full of specialist knowledge and insights into the city.

Just because the city is not currently a topic that is much discussed by legal scholars does not mean that will always be the case. In today's era of *globalization* and *urbanization*, cities are increasingly establishing themselves as global players. As a result, cities are increasingly caught between conflicting national and international interests.

---

15 Weber, Klaus (ed.) (2011), Rechtswörterbuch. Munich, p. 1121. On municipal law, see Tilch, Horst; Arloth, Frank (eds.) (2001), Deutsches Rechts-Lexikon. Vol. 3. Munich, p. 3959. Preuss, Hugo (1906), Die Entwicklung des deutschen Städtewesens. Vol. 1: Entwicklung des deutschen Städtewesens. Leipzig, p. 3, 4, and 5.

It is unlikely that this will not lead to conflicts in which law will, over the short or long term, play a key role. It is hardly going out on a limb to predict that the many legal precedents that once seemed of historical interest alone may be called upon again in the near future. That is currently the law's most important contribution to the topic of the city.

ⓘ *City charters*

German city charters, a legacy of the Middle Ages, build on those laws that were laid down in medieval central Europe, which in turn were influenced by Italian cities and, through them, by the *Roman Empire of antiquity* and, finally, by the city of Rome itself. There, the city was "the centre of all political and social life. The surrounding countryside was no more than an area of dominion and fertile soil to feed the city; whenever culture did develop in the countryside, it had a very urban character. All of culture is urban".[16] At the end of antiquity, this culture collided with the agrarian Germania, the two intermingling in the "great evolutions of the Völkerwanderung".

While, in antiquity, the difference between the city and the countryside was more "economic and quantitative than legal and qualitative", in Germany, cities moved like "oases into the countryside". What was new was that cities were no longer one unit with the surrounding area, but were instead "social and political communities with a shared interest, and as such in conflict with the interests of rural areas".

While in France the medieval city was the "nucleus of the modern city", medieval Germany was a patchwork in which the cities stood out, often forming confederations such as the Hanseatic League, the *League of the Rhine*, or the *Swabian League*. Taken together, this explains why municipal and rural constitutions in Germany differ from one another and why German cities developed their own legal status in the Middle Ages.

The legal scholar *Gerhard Dilcher* provides a succinct description of said status: "a) The city has its own, specifically municipal law that differentiates it from the surrounding area and from ... rural law. b) Furthermore, it can signify that the city is legally defined as a community of citizens, and human interactions in urban society are regulated by legal and not other social norms."

The city distinguishes itself from the countryside – which is why the more liberal "city air makes you free". The regulation of life in the city thus became the precursor to the rule of law. While municipal law is now a thing of the past, the questions linked to the subject are surprisingly topical. They concern the interpretation of the city, its relationship to the surrounding areas and to the state, as well as to other cities or institutions. Thus, municipal law is a collective experience that contains insights and ideas for understanding modernity.

---

16 All quotations in this infobox: Dilcher, Gerhard (1999), Stadtrecht, in: Bader, Karl Siegfried; Dilcher, Gerhard (eds.) (1999), Deutsche Rechtsgeschichte. Land und Stadt – Bürger und Bauer im Alten Europa. Berlin, Heidelberg, New York, p. 1863.

> ℹ️ Berlin (West)
>
> In Berlin, the law became one of the key instruments for securing the city's survival in the *Cold War*. "Berlin" here refers to the unlikely and strange life in the city of Berlin (West) between 1945 and 1990. It owed its existence and survival to an idea, namely that after the end of a murderous war it must be possible to shape a future together, even though the Allies that defeated Nazi Germany had diametrically opposed world views.
>
> After the end of World War II, the USA, the Soviet Union, the United Kingdom, and France put this idea into practice. They occupied Germany and divided it, and the capital city of Berlin, which they controlled together, into four zones. In 1945 and early 1946, the system worked. In 1946, the system began to break down and it was sometimes feared that a new war would break out. Over the years, the former allies were on the brink of starting a war with one another multiple times. Since neither side was willing to budge, the age-old principle of "divide and conquer" won the day. Berlin, Germany, Europe, and the world were divided into East and West. But the division had a blemish. The western sectors of Berlin were adjacent to the city's eastern sectors, but surrounded by the *Soviet occupation zone*. West Berlin literally became an island – politically, economically, and culturally. The legal foundation was the *law of occupation*, which was not rescinded until a generation later in the course of reunification, as unexpected as it was. Seen in detail, Berlin's legal status is one of the most gripping cases in the history of international law. To this day, the law is important in terms of the insights it provides for crisis management:
>
> 1) In a situation that threatens to escalate into war, the more humane and economical solution might be to "freeze" the conflict. A *Cold War* – no matter how debilitating – is still better than a hot one. In a deadlock, diplomacy and law are the most effective instruments for at least diffusing, if not solving, conflicts.
>
> 2) The most innovative legal instrument was the escape clause that allowed the parties to agree to disagree about fundamental issues. These fundamental differences could be separated out – and tolerated – while engaging in dialogue. This *policy of détente* was implemented from the mid-1960s until the 1970s. Despite all its shortcomings, it is perhaps the most important legacy of the history of diplomacy in the 20th century.
>
> 3) The third thing to be learned from this law is that, given the two above-mentioned conditions, what is key is to carefully, even pedantically, and patiently regulate every detail. The treaties and regulations agreed between the East and West about and in Berlin show that it is worth the effort. These details created the foundation for a fragile balance of power to exist at all and left open the possibility of reunification.

7. City as memory space (history)

The historical disciplines are some of the oldest to investigate the city. Two facts are key to this overview: on the one hand, almost all significant historical descriptions of cities have been written by historians; on the other hand, the city as a concept is only an historical instrument in one subdiscipline. While state, national, global, and even social history have been examined as exhaustively as eras or issues, the city is rarely looked at beyond the individual case.

While the city is absent in the methodological and theoretical considerations in this field, it is very present in practice. As in a seek-and-find image, the city often gets lost within the bigger picture, especially when its name is identical with that of the empire associated with it, as in *Babylon, Athens,* or *Rome*.

But the rare systematic historical investigations of the city have yielded substantial results. They, for example, deliver the following answer to the question of what a city is: To be a city, a settlement must exhibit "long-term use, topographical and administrative unity, a variety of structures, as well as a large population as the prerequisite for marked occupational specialization and social differentiation. It must also function as a central hub for the surrounding area, especially in the economic sector".[17] *Size, unity, diversity, permanence, building structure,* and a *central function* are, in this definition, the characteristics that make a city. That is little different from what other disciplines say. In other analyses, urban lifestyle is also sometimes mentioned. The archaeologist *Hans J. Nissen*'s innovative argument that the city is a set of "answers to specific local challenges" has already been cited.

While the above viewpoint results from the study of the city's beginnings, *national and regional history* has made pioneering strides in terms of providing fundamental analyses of the city. The results of a conference at the *Institut für vergleichende Städtegeschichte* (Institute of Comparative Urban History) in *Münster* are a good example of this research. *Alfred Heit* gave an illuminating lecture on the concept of the city at the conference.

Beginning with *Immanuel Kant*, he traced the development of the German concept of the city in the social sciences and humanities. In his insightful interpretations, he found cross-references and reflected on the epistemic agendas of individual authors and schools. Particularly eye-opening were the links Heit found between *Georg von Below, Gustav von Schmoller, Werner Sombart,* and *Max Weber*. In short, according to Heit, von Below's achievement was to integrate criteria identified by historical research into a viewpoint informed by jurisprudence. Schmoller became von Below's adversary and expanded the scope of historical research. He developed one of the most comprehensive definitions of the city. It covered all of the features that remain relevant to this day: *size,*

> Kolb, Frank (2002), Rom. Die Geschichte der Stadt in der Antike. Munich. *A good overview and a good place to start.*
>
> Nissen, Hans J. (2005), Vom Weiler zur Großstadt im frühen Vorderen Orient, in: Falk, Harry (ed.) (2005), Wege zur Stadt. Entwicklung und Formen urbanen Lebens in der alten Welt. Bremen, p. 39–59. *Fundamental.*
>
> Johanek, Peter; Post, Franz-Joseph (eds.) (2004), Vielerlei Städte. Der Stadtbegriff. Cologne. *A conference at the Institute of Comparative Urban History in Münster. Best investigation of the concept of the city.*

---

17 Kolb, Frank (2010), Tatort "Troja". Geschichte, Mythen, Politik. Paderborn, Munich, Vienna, Zurich, p. 280–281. On the term "city", see Heit, Alfred (2004), Vielfalt der Erscheinung – Einheit des Begriffs, Eine Stadtdefinition in der deutschsprachigen Stadtgeschichtsforschung seit dem 18. Jahrhundert, in: Johanek, Peter; Post, Franz-Joseph (eds.) (2004), Vielerlei Städte. Der Stadtbegriff. Cologne, Weimar, Vienna, p. 1–12 (which also cites Schmoller, see the next infobox).

division of labour, market, hub, unit, political and legal relevance. This seemingly universal definition also included the characteristic "intellectual hub", but failed to delineate it further.

> **ⓘ** Gustav von Schmoller's concept of the city
>
> "The city is a larger place to live than the village, but at the same time a place where traffic, trade, industry, and a further division of labour has occurred; a place that no longer grows enough food for all the inhabitants within its boundaries, and that is the economic, administrative, and intellectual focal point for the surrounding rural areas. But one is also reminded that it boasts streets and bridges, a marketplace, town hall, big shops and other larger buildings, that it is more well protected than the village by fortresses, moats, and walls, should such protection actually be necessary, and finally that it possesses a higher political and municipal constitution and certain legal rights."

Werner Sombart, for his part, had another aim. Rather than encyclopaedic completeness or finding a holistic "essence, he sought a functional definition oriented toward modern academic specialization".

Max Weber limited his equally sweeping definition to the concept of the "occidental city", which for him had five features: 1) *fortification*, 2) a *market*, 3) its own court and, at least partially, an autonomous *legal system*, 4) a *communal association* (*Verbandcharakter*) and, concomitantly, 5) at least partial *autonomy*.

His definition thus includes "sovereign, economic, legal, political, administrative, and corporative features". Such an approach has the potential to become a promising method.

Summing up, it is only at first glance that historians do not have a nuanced perception of the city. The discipline of history has done much to better our understanding through both numerous case studies and fundamental methodological work, in particular in the areas of *antiquity* and *regional and national history*.

8. City as hope and disappointment (philosophy)

The arguments put forward by philosophers are even more fundamental. Their view is both encouraging and discouraging. At the beginning – and typically for philosophical explorations of the topic – there is *Aristotle*'s still relevant view of the city as a method of instilling virtue and happiness. For him, city and state are a, if not *the*, means to the end of a "better" life. His reflections are throughout functional, instrumental, and normative. Ever since, philosophical debates on the city have had three main foci:

Political philosophy: Closely connected to *political science*, this branch of philosophy gained its next important impetus from Cicero's *De re publica*. Until the *Middle Ages*, before branching out in the modern era, both Christian and

Islamic philosophers examined the relationship between the state and religion. Nearly all philosophical approaches mix empirical observations with normative assumptions.

Philosophy of law: This subfield is more comprehensive than political philosophy and at the same time closely linked to it, since all philosophy of law is based on assumptions about the city. Exhaustive studies were conducted by *Immanuel Kant, Georg Wilhelm Friedrich Hegel,* and *Johann Gottlieb Fichte* and, in the 20th century, by *Gustav Radbruch, Hans Kelsen,* in questionable ways *Carl Schmitt,* and, more recently and comprehensively, *John Rawls.* This field remains an important area and we are only at the beginning of grasping its relevance for our era of globalization and digital transformation.

The best and least-known standard reference work: Ritter, Joachim; Gründer, Karlfried (eds.) (2007), Historisches Wörterbuch der Philosophie, (1976–2007). Available online at: www.schwabeonline.ch.

Lyotard, Jean-François (1995), Toward the Postmodern. New Jersey. *One of the most influential texts of the past decades, it announced the end of the grand narratives.*

Lefebvre, Henri (2017, original 1968), The Right to the City. New York. *Lefebvre, a Marxist, is one of the few philosophers in the second half of the 20th century to have dealt directly with the city.*

Utopian philosophy is perhaps the most influential and certainly the most colourful subfield of political philosophy. It takes its name from *Thomas Morus*'s 1516 book, *Utopia,* but Ernst Bloch has argued that forward-thinking ideas are much older, and even *Plato*'s ideal city had utopian features. Utopias conjure up dreams – and, preventatively, nightmares – in an attempt to form a better future. Almost always, cities have been used to illustrate these visions. Sometimes entire countries and cities are conjured up and landscapes are often described in detail, but it is in the city that a utopia must pass its stress test. In the early 20th century, optimism about the future was still prevalent in philosophical works. Since then, negative perspectives have been dominant. For *Jean-François Lyotard,* for example, urban living is one of modernity's failed projects. In his depressing view, cities have not delivered on the urban utopia of "culture for the people". Instead, they have become tourist museums of an obsolete way of living. Today's philosophy has no positive utopias to offer; they have become the sole purview of *marketing.*

This has led to one of the peculiarities of philosophical thought. While there is a great tradition of political philosophy, there is no concomitant tradition of urban philosophy. It is, then, no wonder that the discipline does not have its own concept of the city. Three things should be noted in conclusion:

Functional view: Philosophers are not interested in the city as a city. Like the viewpoints we find in sociology, the city is at best a vessel for diagnoses pertaining to society that is used to criticize old concepts, develop new ones, and test them with arguments. Also, as in sociology, philosophy has not yet been able to place the city within a conceptual framework.

Holistic view: One of philosophy's assets is the field's holistic approach.

Normative view: The almost entirely normative viewpoints are also striking. The city is either an ideal, as it was for Aristotle, or a failed experiment, as for

Lyotard – those are the two poles between which investigations move. Yet it is often unclear which criteria are even being applied. In utopian visions this can be inspiring, it becomes in the main a criticism of contemporary conditions. European and North American philosophers often seem like grumpy brothers – they are still predominantly men – within the academic family. Aristotle's emphatic praise of the city as the only place that offers a good life still acts as a reference point, but is overshadowed by disappointed expectations. Still the question remains: What were philosophers hoping for?

The discipline we will next discuss speaks of people's expectations of the city and about how they use this tool. More abstractly, it explores structures, processes, and their impacts.

9. Ways out of no man's land (political science)

📖 Mossberger, Karen; Clarke, Susan E.; John, Peter (eds.) (2012), The Oxford Handbook of Urban Politics. New York. *One of the best manuals currently available.*

Barber, Benjamin R. (2013), If Mayors Ruled the World. Dysfunctional Nations, Rising Cities. New Heaven. *One of the rare political scientists who investigates the relationship between cities and states in a globalized world.*

Sternberger, Dolf (1985), Die Stadt als Urbild. Frankfurt a.M. *Fundamental texts on the city and the state.*

Political science could be the principal activity of urban research, but it is currently of only marginal interest. That was quite different in the late 19th century and, at its peak, it produced influential works of research. Since then, and increasingly since the dominance of the state in the 20th century, interest has shifted to states and governments, and fewer and fewer political scientists are now investigating the city. At the centre of their interest is its function as *community* and *municipality*, which has, for example, been competently and continually researched by *Hiltrud* and *Karl-Heinz Naßmacher* in Germany. But as interesting as their analyses are, they remain limited for two reasons. For one, intensive exploration of the material is necessary to be able to clearly delineate "community" and "municipality". What is more, connections to international issues are dealt with only marginally. Since *international relations* is not a core competency of municipalities, it is rarely investigated. But in the age of *globalization*, this view is limiting. More recent studies in the field have therefore looked at the changing functions of the city. Three examples:

1) Although *Ronan Paddison* is a geographer, his arguments are political in nature. He stresses the role of the modern city as a symbol and its function for the reproduction of the existential bases of societies. These two functions are, in his view, linked, and the symbolic function of the city is dominant in modernity. This thinking represents a major shift from the global city debate. Paddison also focuses on the role of the city as a centre of political control and its ability to live with contradictions and conflicts.[18]

---

18 Paddison, Ronan (2010a), Cities – Revisiting some basics, in: Paddison, Ronan; Timberlake, Michael (eds.) (2010), p. xxvi–xxxi.

A difference to sociological perspectives is evident in this. While the latter sees the city as a mirror of society, Paddison regards it as a pioneering role and in its managerial role. This is true not only on the economic level, as in *Saskia Sassen*'s work, but is most extreme in the areas of policy and culture.

2) *Mike Goldsmith* researches cities in international governmental relations.[19] *Globalization*, regionalization, and regulation have a decisive impact on cities. That is unsurprising. The substantial influence that Goldsmith shows that cities have on the development of the countries in which they are situated, is less obvious. In this way, too, the city is a steering instrument.

3) To better understand this role, *Daniel Kubler* and *Michael A. Pagano* urge us to view "urban politics as multilevel analysis".[20] In doing so, they are promoting a vertical viewpoint that takes into consideration all these issues that impact the state. The authors call this "nesting" and hope to so grasp the complex network and multilinearity in which cities are embedded, making it impossible to reduce them to the local level alone. They complement this vertical view with a horizontal perspective in which all those issues are bundled that affect not only the city itself, but *metropolitan areas*, which often comprise multiple cities.

> **ⓘ** *The post-political city*
>
> The most extreme concept of the city at the time of writing is the "post-political city". This denotes a city "from which true politics have been excised",[21] which refers to the global trend in which real existing capitalism has become so powerful that there is in fact no alternative. Politics then becomes the agent of a sweeping economization of all urban life. This concept, which in the main can be traced back to *Erik Swyngedouw*'s idea of a post-political city in which "a city in which consensus and the principle of a 'purified politics' is privileged and the appropriate spaces/places and institutions are created in which to firmly embed consensus".
>
> At its core, this concept is less about the city and more a critical analysis of politics in general. It is a fundamental critique of the way in which politics is understood today. As such, it has a broader aim than similar approaches such as *austerity urbanism* or the concept of the *neoliberal city*, both of which concentrate on fiscal policy.

As the above examples illustrate, the debate is only just beginning. But it is freeing the city from the constraints of being placed on a level with municipalities and is closing the gap between the municipal and the global. The *Oxford Handbook of Urban Politics* puts it succinctly: "Why should we study urban politics across countries, as we advocate here, when cities are embedded in different national political systems?" The answer: cities are not the same as nation-states.

---

19 Goldsmith, Mike (2012), Cities in intergovernmental systems, in: Mossberger, Karen; Clarke, Susan E.; John, Peter (eds.) (2012), The Oxford Handbook of Urban Politics. New York, p. 133–151.
20 Kübler, Daniel; Pagano, Michael A. (2012), Urban politics as multilevel analysis, in: Mossberger, Karen et al. p. 115–116, p. 120–124.
21 Koch, Philippe; Ross, Beveridge (2018), Postpolitische Stadt, in: Rink, Dieter; Haase, Annegret (eds.) (2018), Handbuch Stadtkonzepte. Analysen, Diagnosen, Kritiken und Visionen. Opladen, p. 279. Mossberger, Karen; Clarke, Susan E.; John, Peter (eds.) (2012), p. 3–4.

The term "*urban politics*" itself may help to establish the city as "a field in its own right" and a separate research area.

Scouring the political sciences to find out how they define a city, it becomes clear that their viewpoint is not very different from that of other disciplines. But political scientists do offer both a holistic perspective and a broad palette of methods and theories. And there is an important difference to sociology: While the differentiation between society and state and between city and other organizational units is problematic, in the political sciences there is a longer tradition of analyses of similar actors, structures, processes, and impacts in almost all areas.

What is more important is the discipline's focus on action. While it is individuals that give personal acts a meaning, these acts become social as soon as other people are affected. This is a key difference between sociology and political science. While the former looks at social relationships as a whole, the latter is interested in these relationships only when conflicts can no longer be resolved on the personal level. Every societal action may be social, but not everything that is social is also political. However, everything that is social can become political when conflicts arise that can only be settled outside of personal relationships.

Unlike the *village*, the city is a place that is typical for such conflicts. Cities are always at least to some extent anonymous, because of their size alone everybody does not know everybody else. In any number of contexts, encounters and actions can suddenly become political. They then become interesting because they then have to be regulated. Actors initiate processes that either confirm or change structures, which in turn leads to feedback loops and perhaps to further steps.

In sum, political science is one of the most important disciplines for understanding and describing the city. Even if current research is still too much focused on the municipal level, it offers promising approaches.

10. The city: a puzzle

Against all expectations, there is some consensus when it comes to the results presented by the key disciplines. Scholars in all fields agree that it is not possible to define the city – and then immediately ignore their own claim. The definitions that scholars in various fields have suggested all contain the features of a) *density* and b) *diversity*. That is more than is to be expected, but is insufficient to completely grasp what a city is. And beyond this lowest common denominator the differences begin.

The most sweeping viewpoints can be found in the oldest and the youngest disciplines. *Philosophical* thought focuses on the question of what a city should be. Its topics are the "good life" as well as the city as a "master tool" for achieving this life; disappointed expectations are often presented in anti-utopias (*dystopias*).

Urbanity, the core concept of *urbanism*, is unspecific and contested. The jury is still out on whether it can establish itself as a discipline in the long term, or whether use of the term will prove to be no more than a fad.

The fields that have investigated the city most exhaustively are *sociology* and *urban sociology*. Currently, sociologists have the prerogative of interpretation. Sociologists concentrate on *density* and *diversity* and their consequences. But their explorations are limited on account of not clearly defining the relationship between city and society.

Modern theories of space link both of the above disciplines with *geography* and *urban geography*. To explain what a city is, (urban) geographers have created a comprehensive catalogue of features. While they describe geographical *urban space*, *urban ecologists* research *natural spaces* in urban areas. Their main interest is in the city as an ecosystem, with a particular emphasis on human beings' ecological footprint. While these disciplines focus on analyzing existing conditions, *urban* and *spatial planning* and *architecture* are concerned with their division and design. In so doing, they have developed manifold forms.

In economics and *law*, the city is today a marginal subject. Yet these disciplines look back on a rich tradition of influential concepts, particularly in the areas of *urban economics* and *municipal law*. Although these topics are seldom discussed today, legal scholars have a repertoire of experience they can draw from at any time.

For *historians* – who think mainly in terms of eras, regions, and issues – the city lies crosswise. In contrast to large institutions like empires or states, there have been few systematic explorations of the city. This leads to a peculiar paradox. While historians are responsible for almost all biographies of cities and have researched their beginnings extensively, providing key foundational concepts in the process, they have not provided a clearly delineated concept of the city itself.

Finally, in the *political sciences*, the focus has been and still is on municipal policy. The hierarchical thinking prevalent in their discipline has similarities to economics and law. But that should not determine our view of the field. New approaches and concepts such as *urban politics* and *urban governance* are embarking on a promising path.

What do we now know when we review these insights? How do they answer the question of "For which problem is the city a solution?" From a scientific point of view, we do not, ultimately, know what a city is. There is no one overarching definition used by all disciplines. This is another paradox, for, on the one hand, the city is the oldest tool for helping a large number of human beings to live together, on the other hand, numerous authors believe it impossible to define the concept definitively owing to its complexity. This is hardly convincing, as scientists have had no problem defining much more complex phenomena than the city. But do we even need to know what a city is? There are two arguments that strongly suggest that we do.

1) A large part of urban research is taken up with the description of terms, concepts, and city types. We now know a great many of these, most of them quite exactly. But we do not have a benchmark against which to measure their relevance. If we could say what we mean by *the* city, we would be able to make an informed judgement. That is important if only for the reason that individual cities are often oriented towards ideals of city types, for example the *smart city*, without which modern urban planning seems incapable of working.
2) Furthermore, if, for example, *Saskia Sassen*'s description of the global city is convincing and this type of city is a network with its own dynamics, that would have an explosive impact. Sociologists would have to not only pose the question anew of what the relationship is between society and the city, but also to look at this relationship in a globalized world. This is even more far-reaching for scholars of *international relations*. States have not lost their relevance, but their role has shifted. Today there are numerous players that are threatening the status of the nation-state. What, only a generation ago, was linked to the term "sovereignty" is now limited and there is almost no place left on this planet where national decisions are without a broader influence owing to global interdependencies. Finding a place for the global city within this system seems barely possible. In the field of *international relations*, the city is not a player but, in reality, it is. For that reason alone, it is more critical than ever to answer the question of what we understand by a city.

Table 2. The concept of the city in different disciplines

DISCIPLINE	CONCEPT OF CITY	ESSENCE	STRENGTHS	WEAKNESSES
Urbanism	No concept of its own, some urbanists even question their own discipline	CORE TERMS: - Urbanity (urban lifestyle) MODES OF THOUGHT: - Levels	- Interdisciplinary - Integrative - Incorporates new methods - Empirical	- No own methods - Core term polysemous and contested - Problem of the multilevel approach
(Urban) sociology	Influential concepts (Sombart, Weber, Park, Wirth, Sassen etc.) - Dominance of structural/functional viewpoints - Features: - Size | density - Stability - Market - Fortification - Private – public - Division of labour - Production/services, esp. for surrounding area - Transport network - Separation of functions (e.g. living and working) - Dominance of small households - Rationality - High social mobility - Many city types	CORE TERMS: - Society - Density - Diversity MODES OF THOUGHT: - Structural - Action-oriented approaches - Few links between the two approaches	- Most in-depth study of the topic - Plurality of concepts - Numerous different approaches	- Boundary between city and society blurry and contested - Metaphor of the city as segment, mirror, image, synonym of society - Diagnosed the phenomenon of the global city but has not integrated it into the discipline as a whole - Only partially recognizes the political dimension of the global city - Problem of the multilevel approach
Economics	Features of urban economics: - Opposition city–country - Size - Density - Division of labour is spatial - Dependent on political rulers, societal organizations, form of production	CORE TERMS: - Urban economics - Municipal economy - Markets - Sites of activities (e.g. working, living, transportation) - Infrastructure MODES OF THOUGHT: - Structural	- Historical importance of urban economics	- Link between globalization, global cities, and their relevance for the economy only partially grasped - Relationship public–private, state–economy–city unclear - Problem of the multilevel approach

DISCIPLINE	CONCEPT OF CITY	ESSENCE	STRENGTHS	WEAKNESSES

(Urban) geography/ urban/spatial planning	- Spatial/functional concept of the city
	- Distances itself from general, encyclopaedic concepts of the city
	- General features:
	  • Unity (administrative)
	  • City charters
	  • Size (population)
	  • Density (inhabitants)
	  • Labour structure
	- Features across cultures, eras, and religions:
	  • Closed settlement with a centre
	  • Urban house styles
	  • Density of buildings (increases towards the centre)
	  • Diversity
	  • Inner differentiation
	  • Traffic situation
	  • Concentration of non-agricultural workplaces
	- Features of urban geography:
	  • Function as hub
	  • Centre of transportation and innovation
	  • Urban lifestyle
	  • Secondary and tertiary economy
	- Spatial features:
	  • Built around a centre
	  • Differences between centre and margins
	  • Closed building style
	  • Creation of neighbourhoods
	  • Dense infrastructure
	  • City = main force in organization of population
	  • Dynamic urban system
		CORE TERMS:
		- Urban space
		- Density
		- Centralization/ hub
		- Relationship city–surroundings
		
		MODES OF THOUGHT:
		- Structural
		- Levels/layers
			- Great awareness of complexity of the concept
			- Nuanced
			- Many criteria
				- Distrust of general concepts of the city
				- Geographical concept blurry
				- Criteria are not always prioritized the same way
				- Criteria are not brought into context
				- Difficult to localize the global city (seen to represent movement of money, not people)
				- Phenomenon of the "collapse of space"
				- Problem of the multilevel approach

DISCIPLINE	CONCEPT OF CITY	ESSENCE	STRENGTHS	WEAKNESSES

Urban planning/ architecture	− Reflection of society
	− No concept specific to the discipline
	− Features:
	  • Legal status
	  • Power
	  • Fortification
	  • Division of labour
	  • Commuters
	  • Lifestyle
	  • Complexity
		CORE TERMS:
		− Urban planning
		− Urban space
		
		MODES OF THOUGHT:
		− Structural
		− Levels
		− Layers
		− Processes
			− Awareness of complexity of the concept
			− Very knowledgeable about the spatial organization of cities
			− Normative concepts
				− Practice without a specific concept
				− Problem of the multilevel approach

Law	− No concept specific to the discipline
	− City = term for municipalities
	− General features:
	  • Size
	  • Slanted towards business
	  • City charters
	  • Opposition village–countryside
	− Currently in Germany:
	  • Municipality = lowest level of polity
	  • No independent law for cities
	  • Right of self-government
	− City charters (historical)
	  • Centre of political life
	  • Dominance over countryside (= agriculture, dominion)
	− Cities do not form a unit with the countryside
		CORE TERMS:
		− Municipality
		− State
		− City charters
		
		MODES OF THOUGHT:
		− Structural
		− Levels
		− Processes
		− Historical development
			− Large repertoire of specialized knowledge about central problems:
			− Citizens of the city/country
			− City charters/constitutional law/municipal law
			− City as an international problem/international law
				− Relevance of the city only recently beginning to be reflected in current legal system
				− Problem of the multilevel approach

History	− Criteria
	  • Size
	  • Closed unit
	  • Market
	  • Legal standing
	  • Autonomy
	  • Division of labour
	  • Social differentiation
	  • Diversity of buildings
	  • Urban lifestyle
	  • Function as hub
	  • Infrastructure
	− City functions as platform or object
	− Subject
		− Eras
		− Regions
		− Issues
			− Fundamental knowledge of the birth of cities (esp. through *archaeology*)
			− Numerous portraits of cities
			− Fundamental knowledge of antiquity
			− Conceptual history of *regional and national histories*
				− City is a subcategory of or synonym for states or empires
				− Problem of the multilevel approach

DISCIPLINE	CONCEPT OF CITY	ESSENCE	STRENGTHS	WEAKNESSES
Philosophy	− No concept specific to the discipline − Normative, functionalist viewpoint − City is a tool for the "good life"	CORE TERMS/ MODES OF THOUGHT: − The good life	− City as an achievement of civilization − City as utopia and dystopia	− Wavers between hope and disappointment − Philosophy of the state, but not of the city

Political science	− Urban politics
	− Urban governance
	− Structural, functionalist viewpoint
	− Concept related to municipal policy:
	  • Large settlement
	  • Self-governing
	  • Based on trade, commerce, and industry
	  • Branched structure
	  • Density/concentration (construction by productive, administrative, and cultural institutions)
	  • Autonomous political administration of an area
	− Relationship city–surroundings
		CORE TERMS:
		− Municipal politics
		− Urban politics
		
		MODES OF
		THOUGHT:
		− Levels
		− Structures
		− Actors
		− Processes
		− Feedback loops
			− Delineation state–city
			− Governance as problem-solving approach
			− Potential to solve the problem of the multilevel approach
			− Potential to become leading discipline
			− Debate on the limits of past approaches
				− Problem of the multilevel approach
				− City is a subcategory of or synonym for states or empires
				− Not yet able to place the global city phenomenon in context

B. The grand narratives

Although scholars from various disciplines have provided diverse answers to what the essence of a city is, this overview so far lacks a definition. What we need to do is sharpen our focus. That is what experts have done throughout the ages. In a kind of speed dating, let us ask them what they think, not forgetting, of course, that a large body of literature exists by and on each scholar. We are only interested in their answer to one question: Which problem does the city solve? – Date #1:

1. The good city (Aristotle)

Our very first author is a standout. For the ancient Greek philosopher *Aristotle*, the city provided *the* opportunity for "the good life". That for him made it not only civilization's greatest achievement, but also a tool for the education, preparation, and improvement of human beings so that they may develop into "better" and "higher" beings. This early assessment continues to reverberate to this day. *Aristotle*'s argument is normative, which is strange as it would be more fitting for *Plato*. Since he was an empiricist, one would expect an encyclopaedic exploration of the city from Aristotle. But he did provide a few suggestions for planning a city in terms of buildings, health, and air flow, as well as fortifications for defence, water supply, and beauty. He also believed that a city needed a representative sacred building and a marketplace. That is, no doubt, all important, but is not embedded within a system and would have been long forgotten were it not for his view of the city as a tool, which has been so powerful for more than two and a half millennia. This idea fascinates people to this day. Aristotle's answer to the question of what a city is is clear: It is a tool for a "better life".

> [i] *Aristotle's promise*
> "That which lifted human beings above the conditions of barbarism, in which they are no more than economic beings, that which made it possible for them to develop their higher abilities, which only lay dormant in the age of barbarism, namely to live well and virtuously rather than simply to live, was his participation in and membership of a city. A person's physical and animal being might be satisfied in the countryside, but his intellectual needs can only be satisfied in the city."[22]

A less normative and more analytical and descriptive picture of the city is found in the modern social sciences, primarily sociology. In this area, it is impossible to avoid *Max Weber*'s or *Georg Simmel*'s ideas. *Werner Sombat*, by contrast, is rarely drawn upon. That is surprising, since he has provided one of the most comprehensive and systematic ideas, while Weber's text on the city is only a posthumous fragment and Simmel's contribution is limited to one essay.

---

22   Hotzan, Jürgen (1994), dtv-Atlas zur Stadt. Tafeln und Texte. Von den ersten Gründungen bis zur modernen Stadtplanung. Munich, p. 25. See Aristotle, Politics, VII:11 (classics.mit.edu/Aristotle/politics.html).

2. The multifunctional city (Werner Sombart)

Werner Sombart's understanding of the city is universal. He does not limit himself either in time or space – thus setting himself apart from almost all other scholars. "The objective conditions [for the foundation of a city] can ... be of very many kinds: having to do with climate, construction, transportation, economics, population, and who knows what else!"[23] This sweeping viewpoint is notable, because from the beginning he does not limit himself to his own discipline. That makes it easier to understand why Sombart not only names a handful but a dozen features that characterize this form of human community. Sombart is one of only few scholars who fulfil today's demand for interdisciplinarity. A sociologist and an economist, Sombart's method is interesting. He derived functions by stressing the diversity that is typical for the city. By so doing, he broke down the concept of the city, making it easier to grasp. The advantage is that the features of the city, the individual pieces of the puzzle are made visible. The disadvantage is that this does not come together to provide an overview. It is unclear how the pieces of the puzzle fit together. Nevertheless, he developed a relatively clear picture: for Sombart, the city organizes diversity.

Table 3. Sombart's aspects of the city

ASPECT	EXPLANATION
Sacral	City as the place where the gods live; in Christianity, the see; in other religions, the site of the temple
Military	Cities as walled settlements: fortresses, garrisons
Architectural	"A conglomerate of buildings without regard to the inhabitants"
Population	The inhabitants of a place without regard to the buildings
Size, density	"Continuous concentration of people and human dwellings"
Geographical	"…that covers a considerable piece of land"
Climatic	Dependent on the region's climate
Transportation	At important transport hubs
Economic	"Settlement of people who are dependent on external agricultural production for their sustenance"
Sociological	Settlement in which the inhabitants no longer all know each other
Political	Seat of political institutions
Legal	Settlement that enjoys privileges

---

23 Sombart, Werner (2005, original 1902), Der Moderne Kapitalismus. Vol. 2. Munich, p. 189–190. See also Sombart, Werner (1931), Siedlungen. II. Städtische Siedlung. Stadt, in: Vierkandt, Alfred (ed.) (1931), Handwörterbuch der Soziologie. Stuttgart, p. 527–532.

3. Politics, the market, and city types (Max Weber)

Max Weber took a different approach. Strictly speaking, he had two ideas and never clearly came down in favour of one or the other. His investigation of the topic begins with a harmless list of features. The city, according to Weber, is "… a (at least relatively) closed settlement … [and a] … large locality. … The city is a settlement the inhabitants of which live primarily off trade and commerce rather than agriculture … [and] the local inhabitants satisfy an economically substantial part of their daily needs on the local market, and essentially by products which the local population or that of the immediate hinterland produced for sale in the market or acquired in other ways."[24]

There are two situations that lead to the formation of a city in Weber's view. Either the "presence of a feudal estate or a market. The economic and political needs of a feudal or princely estate can encourage specialization". Or there is a "regular rather than an occasional exchange of goods [and] the market becomes an essential component in the livelihood of the settlers".

Hence, the economy is responsible for the emergence of the city. But two things have to happen in a specific order: production and then regular trade. In other words, the city is a market.

In a closer reading of Weber's text, his introduction to his main argument is striking. He mentions the need for the "presence of a feudal estate" at its core. It is easy to overlook this, since the sentence goes on to stress economic functions as the main feature. But this aside contains an eminently important core. Weber speaks of the city as a centre of power. That is both a spatial and a political argument. The city is a political instrument of power for structuring and having control over space, and not only a market. For Weber, politics was the prerequisite for a market to actually be able to function in the long term.

Weber names further features of the city, such as its forms of association, *autonomy* (both political arguments), and an independent legal system. Such diversity explains why he saw the city as its own form of settlement and why he did not equate urban society with society in general. All in all, Weber's understanding of the city is modern, nuanced, and dynamic. In the main he was thinking of the *medieval European city*, which for him was the ideal type.[25]

That brings us to his method: "Weber's method is to create what he calls an 'ideal type' of social structures like the city, then to explore why reality diverges from the model".[26] It is hardly surprising that the former did not cut a good figure in Weber's sceptical worldview. From here, two paths can be taken. It is possible to conduct concrete empirical research on case studies. Or, and this is the path that Weber chose, one can make an attempt at an overview, which Weber achieved by sorting manifold developments into types. This method, already practised by *Sombart*, became and remains to this day the gold standard

---

24   Weber, Max (2000), p. 1–2. Nippel, Wilfried (2000), p. 126–130. The following quotations: ibid., p. 66.
25   Koch, Florian (2011), p. 88–90.
26   Sennett, Richard (2018), p. 61.

of urban research and has led to a tremendous expansion of the semantic content of "the city". The debate has become broad rather than deep.

As differentiated as Weber's picture of the city was, his Eurocentric perspective and his ignorance of players are by now outdated. It also remains a mystery why a scholar with such a universal education and a solid foundation in *antiquity* failed to discuss *Aristotle*'s idea of the *polis* as a tool for a good life. This can perhaps be explained by the fact that Weber was searching for something else. His passion was to explain the fall of the *Roman Empire*. There is no escaping the city, since the empire was an urban civilization with a differentiated system of cities. Nevertheless, Weber could have come across Aristotle's idea, at least in reference to the importance of people. In fact, he must have, for example in *Cicero*'s work, which was heavily influenced by Greek philosophy. The best form of government for the good life of human beings – who do not appear in Weber's work, he did not want to encourage a normative turn in sociology. Our next two urban research pioneers – Dates #4 and #5 – were very concerned with human lives: the sociologist Georg Simmel and the legendary *Chicago School* under *Louis Wirth*.

4. The blasé city dweller (Georg Simmel)

Logic, the history of philosophy, ethics, social psychology, and sociology – philosopher and sociologist *Georg Simmel* was a Renaissance man with an inexhaustible curiosity. His house in *Berlin-Westend* was an intellectual meeting place, and *Rainer Maria Rilke, Sabine* and *Reinhold Lepsius*, and *Marianne* and *Max Weber* were frequent guests. Simmel published 15 major works and more than 200 essays. His most important work on urban sociology was a short essay written for an exhibition in *Dresden*. The subject matter of the text, published in 1903, is idiosyncratic. Simmel was interested in the *density* of the *big city* and its consequences. At that point in time, many cities were expanding and the size of their population was larger than anything known before. This resulted in a '"feeling of compression" as *Richard Sennett* describes this phenomenon, which had already been the subject of *Gustave Le Bon*'s *Psychology of Crowds*, published eight years previously.

---

[i] *The blasé big-city dweller*

"It is at first the consequence of those rapidly shifting stimulations of the nerves which are thrown together in all their contrasts and from which it seems to us the intensification of metropolitan intellectuality seems to be derived. On that account it is not likely that stupid persons who have been hitherto intellectually dead will be blasé. Just as an immoderately sensuous life makes one blasé because it stimulates the nerves to their utmost reactivity until they finally can no longer produce any reaction at all, so, less harmful stimuli, through the rapidity and the contradictoriness of their shifts, force the nerves to make such violent responses, tear them about so brutally that they exhaust their last reserves of strength and, remaining in the same milieu, do not have time for new reserves to form."[27]

---

27   Simmel, Georg (1984), p. 192–204.

Simmel diagnosed an overstimulation of the senses. For him, one of the main features of the large city was "the intensification of emotional life due to the swift and continuous shift of external and internal stimuli". This caused big city dwellers to become what Simmel called "blasé". The term may sound dated, but it could describe stressed-out hipsters complaining that they are so on edge that they are incapable of reacting emotionally. This blasé outlook has an important function. Simmel sees it as a mask that shields the wearer from sensory overload. One result is that urban residents must at least sometimes be able to retreat into a more manageable, familiar environment. Even though we use different terminology today, Simmel identified one of the key features of a city: the close *proximity* to a large number of other, often very different, people.

To which question is the city the answer? For Simmel, it is a phenomenon caused by modern, capitalist society. We might expect an infinite chain of further conflicts to follow from this diagnosis. But that would not go far enough, for Simmel was only "considering people being in public, moving along a street, having no productive relation to others through whom they move".[28] But the city is also a place in which many very different kinds of people work together in large numbers. Sociality can occur when people are "doing something productive together".

Population density and its impacts are one of the central topics around cities. It is Simmel who must be credited with being the first to provide a succinct and memorable discussion of this topic. Since then, it has often been thematized, for example by Simmel's student *Lewis Wirth*.

5. The dense city (Lewis Wirth and the Chicago School)

Lewis Wirth was the student not only of Simmel, but also of the influential sociologist *Robert Ezra Park*, co-founder of the *Chicago School*. To this day, Wirth's 1938 essay, "Urbanism as a Way of Life", is often cited. He aimed at a theoretical concept of modernity and the avenues it offers for social integration and participation.

The city was the ideal field in which to find answers. Such motivation is typical for many urban researchers. While this has been the source of much new knowledge, it contains a fundamental problem: These researchers are, in actual fact, not interested in the city itself, but in the developments of their times. Beginning with Karl Marx and Friedrich Engels, that meant the causes and effects of the *industrial revolution* and capitalism, for later scholars it meant the many phases of modernity.

---

28 Sennett, Richard (2018), p. 321. Wirth, Louis (1938), Urbanism as way of life, Digital version: uc.edu/cdc/oldwebsite/fall03-readings/Urbanism_as_a_way.pdf (accessed: 23 Apr. 2022). In his studies, Wirth takes a critical look at Weber, Simmel, and Sombart, but in the main follows ideas put forward by Ferdinand Tönnies, John Dewey and, in particular, his teacher, Robert Ezra Park, and the Chicago School, to which he belongs.

Friedrich Engels produced one of the most notable descriptions of the 19th-century city; *Karl Marx* drew on this for his fundamental criticism of capitalism and communism; *Ferdinand Tönnies* sought to understand the underlying mechanism of modern communization and was the first to describe the dualism of community and society. *Georg Simmel* analysed the money economy. Werner Sombart conducted a well-founded analysis of capitalism, and *Max Weber* searched for the origins of Occidental capitalism and the phenomenon of communization.

None of these authors was interested in the city per se. And yet it appears as an object of research again and again, for it is in the city that the phenomena they were interested in can best be observed. The city thus came to be seen as a mirror of society – a perspective with far-reaching consequences.

Wirth is in this tradition of scholars who saw the city mostly as a spatial and structural laboratory of society and of modernity. However, he went one step further, consolidating this understanding into a definition. For him, the city is "a relatively large, dense, and permanent settlement of socially heterogeneous individuals".

Unlike *Aristotle*, who understands the city normatively and functionally as a tool, and in contrast to Weber, for whom the city is a politically constituted market, Wirth was interested in immediate interdependencies. While he did not prioritize the four core features of the city he identified – *size*, *density*, *continuity*, and *heterogeneity* – it is clear from his essay that, following Simmel, he believed the latter two to be the constitutive features of the city. As a formula, this can be expressed as: city = dense heterogeneity of a relatively large size. In this way, Wirth identified the city as its own form of community, a result he had not in fact been searching for.

This also led Wirth to a new methodology. Prioritizing heterogeneity means focusing on social differences. This means that not only structures, but also human actions become the main field of inquiry. The explosive power of Wirth's work can be seen in its lasting echo. *Hartmut Häußermann* and *Walter Siebel*, for example, criticized Wirth two generations later as a representative of the theory that defines the city "as a universal and ahistorical fact independent of society."[29] In so doing, they claim, he failed to recognize "the social causes of his observations". What happens in large cities is not an essential form of *large cities*, but – like the city as a form of settlement itself – a consequence of social changes, mainly capitalist industrialization. These create the large city and, concomitantly, urban lifestyles in all its manifestations. Häußermann and Siebel give a clear answer to the question of whether the city or society is the relevant research object: "The city is not an independent variable ... [it] is no longer the cause of social developments, but provides a stage for them."

This critique makes the focus of the debate clear: Is the city a subject or an object? But while that puts it in a nutshell, it detracts from the broader picture.

---

29 Häußermann, Hartmut; Siebel, Walter (2004), p. 93, p. 96, and p. 100.

There is no question that "city" and "society" are interdependent, nor did Wirth claim the opposite. The question is not *whether* they are, but *how*.

Yet this question cannot be answered abstractly. The true problem is the manner in which it is repeatedly posed. The artificiality of this viewpoint becomes clear if we change perspectives. In political and historical approaches, it has often been shown that cities have had different functions at different times and can be stage and object as well as subject and even actor. The debate among sociologists is so intense because of a fundamental contradiction in sociological discussions of the city. The metaphorical description as "mirror", "hotspot", or "stage" of societal life, particularly in modernity, leads to an intellectual dead end if there is no definition of what is meant by "city" and "society". If the city is part of society, it can be understood as an independent unit. If the city is a mirror of society, then the mirrored unit is one and the same with society, making an independent concept of the city unnecessary.

Ironically, critics of Wirth attack his work at the point at which it was most innovative. He may have been overextending the concept of "city" by seeing it as a mirror of both society and modernity, but he deserves credit for not quite trusting the popular metaphor of the mirror. This led him to a more nuanced definition. The roots of his arguments can already be found in the work of his teacher, *Robert Ezra Park*, who stated emphatically: "The city is not … merely a physical mechanism and an artificial construction. It is involved in the vital processes of the people who compose it; it is a product of nature and particularly of human nature."[30] The *Chicago School* was very clear on which problem the city is a solution for.

Their focus on the role of human beings represented a shift in perspective. Behaviour and actions became more important than structures. That perspective was the school's great innovation. Although that, in fact, answered the question of whether it is necessary to distinguish between society and urban society, debates on the question raged among another two generations of sociologists, most radically in the work of *Jürgen Friedrichs*.

6. No city (Jürgen Friedrichs)

Jürgen Friedrichs insisted that the concept of the "city" should be abandoned. Even though he later qualified his approach, his three main arguments are worth exploring:

1) The city is a "social laboratory" in which social issues are concentrated under a magnifying glass. Any analysis of the city is therefore an analysis of society and cannot be justified as the sole focus of research.

---

30 Park, Robert Ezra; Burgess, Ernest Watson (1992, original 1925), The City. Suggestions for Investigation of Human Behaviour in the Urban Environment. Chicago, London, p. 1.

2) The city has yet to be convincingly defined. It is too general a term, making any search for a definition redundant.
3) Ever-greater specialization has replaced a holistic view. That development truncated the tradition of macrosociology, and no synthesis of traditions is in sight.

"Since the city is literally the place where social analysis is conducted," Friedrichs therefore wrote, "one might come to the conclusion that the city is not an area in the field of sociology that can be delimited."[31] Rather than a theory of the city, what was needed was a "general theory of the interplay of social and spatial organizations".

As long as we accept the metaphors of a "laboratory", "mirror", or "hotspot" of modernity, these arguments are solid. But so are the counterarguments, of which the strongest nullifies Friedrichs's position: The mirror metaphor denotes the idea that society is too complex to grasp completely, making it necessary to look at a representative cross-section. But if that were so, there would be no difference between city and society. That would make it impossible to explain why so many people continue to move to cities. Equating city and society would mean that the city is not an answer, because no question has been asked. Not a very convincing argument.

If, ultimately, Friedrichs wanted to do away with the city as an analytical category, two decades later a new revolutionary hypothesis shocked the world of urban research.

7. The global city (Saskia Sassen)

The sociologist and economist *Saskia Sassen* did not reject the concept of the city, but radically redefined it. The shockwaves that her research produced reverberated far beyond the field of urbanism and continue to do so to this day.

The development that Sassen described began in the 1980s. When the *Big Bang* – the deregulation of international financial markets in London in 1986 – happened a new situation was created that Sassen sought to understand. Up until that point, the city had been situated firmly below the state. International interrelations had at times been thematized, but nobody ever had the idea of examining all the consequences this had for the city. In her theory of the global city *Saskia Sassen* proposed a thesis to which economists and political scientists have still not been able to respond adequately. She showed that many cities – especially *New York City*, *London*, and *Tokyo* – act as global cities and are more powerful and influential than most states.

---

31 Friedrichs, Jürgen (1977), p. 17 and p. 19.

> ⓘ **Paradigm shift**
>
> "Sociologists have tended to study cities by looking at the ecology of human forms and the distribution of population and institutional centres or by focusing on people and social groups, lifestyles, and urban problems. These approaches are no longer sufficient."[32]

Sassen's approach was fundamentally new. For her, the city was "one particular site in which global processes take place". A key proposition, which regards the city as a platform for *globalization*. But if we follow this idea through to the end, the global city is even more than that. It becomes the subject, an international player.

The theory must be credited with placing globalization in context. The global economy does not exist "somewhere out there outside the nation-states," but in the metropolises of the world market. These are characterized by four functions: They are 1) highly concentrated command centres for organizing the world economy, 2) key locations for financial markets and services as well as the corresponding companies, 3) production sites and locations for innovations by leading industries, and 4) important markets for these products.

The ensuing discussion of Sassen's work branched out in multiple directions. Perhaps most influential was the attempt to identify global cities and understand their relevance. That led to a number of differentiations, for example into first- and second-tier global cities and a concomitant ranking. The process of hierarchization is easy to grasp and is most likely the reason it is so effective.

A second area of exploration delved into the question of why administrative and geographical borders almost never converge. This is true of most cities and is not a new phenomenon. The solution to this problem was found in the concept of the *region*, which led to the coining of the term "*global city region*".

A third line of research sought to pinpoint the topic through an analysis of individual branches.

The most important contributions to this discussion emerged from the field of sociology. It is notable that both political scientists and economists were much less present when it came to the reception of Sassen's work. That is surprising given that Sassen's theory challenges the core of political science, in which nation-states still play the leading role. A first reaction to Sassen was to link her ideas to the concept of governance. Just as networks became the leading concept over structure, politics became governance. But is that a convincing argument?

If we understand structure to be static and politics as more or less the purview of the nation-state, then this new viewpoint seems justified. But structures are not only static and politics is not exclusively governmental. To reduce pol-

---

32 Sassen, Saskia (1997, original 1994), Metropolen des Weltmarkts. Die neue Rolle der Global Cities. Frankfurt a.M., New York, p. 9–11 and p. 3. Bronger, Dirk (2004), Metropolen, Megastädte, Global Cities. Die Metropolisierung der Erde. Darmstadt, p. 145–149.

itics to only a national government, thereby ignoring lobby work and interest groups, for instance, reflects neither today's reality nor the past. Here, at the latest, a similarity can be made out. As strong as Sassen's concept of the global city is, its description and delineation are strangely unmodern.

This becomes clear if we subject her model to a historical countercheck. Can the idea of "commando centres of the global economy" be applied to other eras, for example *antiquity* or the *Middle Ages*? Naturally there was, at that time, no global commerce in today's sense, but there was a great deal of trade with far-away places. We could, for example, use Sassen's terminology to describe the economic role played by ancient *Rome*.[33] And *Florence* under the Medici can be interpreted as *the* key centre of the early modern money economy. Finally, *London* and *Berlin* were important production sites and markets for the innovative industries of the 19th century, which brought forth new products and branches of industry, for example the locomotives produced by the global leader Borsig or products made by AEG and Osram. Max Weber would have been thrilled by Sassen's theory.

But what distinguishes ancient *Rome* from global cities like *New York City* today is not the role of a highly concentrated commando centre, but their dimensions, the scope of their influence, and the effectiveness of the innovative tools of the digital revolution. And, above all, their momentum or the accelerated pace at which they fulfil their functions. In this sense, the global city also stands for a shifting of power to very few cities. While global cities are becoming powerful actors on the international stage, there is a bitter flipside to this development, namely marginalized cities and regions and decelerated zones such as the *shrinking city*. The global city, to summarize Sassen's answer to our initial question, is the urban answer to *globalization*.

The construct of the concept of the global city has been one of the most innovative and influential scholarly achievements of recent decades. It created an awareness of the city and its relevance for the global economy. Nevertheless, this approach concentrates on one particular function, which is legitimate, but pushes other functions out of the focus of attention. This has increasingly been challenged. Date #8, for example, wants to bring the debate back to Earth.

8. The ordinary city (Ash Amin and Stephen Graham)

The concept of the *ordinary city* is not meant to counter the *global city* or other city typologies, but is against methods that unduly stress individual functions. That, in a nutshell, is the view of geographers *Ash Amin* and *Stephen Graham*. They criticise the dominance of economics, which pushes multifunctionality and diversity into the background. That which makes a city what it is thus becomes a secondary characteristic. Amin and Graham see that as a misinterpretation.

---

33   Kolb, Frank (2002), Rom. Die Geschichte der Stadt in der Antike. Munich, p. 250–308.

In their view, cities are spaces of diversity and mixing. "The contemporary city is a variegated and multiplex entity – a juxtaposition of contradictions and diversities, the theatre of life itself. The city is not a unitary or homogeneous entity, and perhaps it has never been this."[34] This statement contains two powerful arguments.

First, it can be read as a modern interpretation of *Georg Simmel*. In this tradition, cities are both "symbols of wealth creation, domination, and opportunity as they are of pollution, poverty, and struggle for survival."[35]

Second, the authors insist that a city is also a unit. However, that does not mean it is homogeneous, but rather a place that holds *heterogeneity* together. This makes their position close to that of sociologist *Gerd Held*. At the centre of Held's explorations is what he calls the "inclusion–exclusion mechanism". He uses it to denote the opportunities available for accessing a variety of social spaces and milieus. The focus is thus on permeability, proximity, and diversity.

Amin and Graham observe two processes in particular. For one, *globalization* goes hand in hand with an intensification of contact due to modern means of communication and the expansion of transportation. This impacts all of daily urban life, which increasingly impacts events in far-away places. Furthermore, it creates a new *layer* between cities, their surroundings, and the world. This layer makes it possible to extend relations, which take on a new, key function as a dynamic platform. Amin and Graham recognize the same phenomena that Sassen and others describe: cities have an influence far beyond their borders, often even on a global level. But Amin and Graham also criticize the method that ascribes only *one* main function to cities. Instead, they propose five:

1) *Proximity:* By this they mean the simultaneous relations between various phenomena in a world of fast flows. This encompasses both spatial propinquity and the ability to be close to far-away developments through, for example, digital channels. Whether real or virtual, cities are meeting places.
2) *Density:* This urban feature, mentioned by almost all authors, is also pinpointed by Amin and Graham. They, however, emphasize its uniqueness and "dense creativity," which they understand as islands or enclaves that have an impact beyond local urban spaces.
3) *Heterogeneity*: Of the many aspects of this key feature, they stress the "contingency of diverse processes".
4) *Nodes:* This term stresses the role of cities as sites of experience with varying spatial and temporal contingencies. It is a result of the layering of various nodes of relations with different rhythms and impacts.

---

34 Amin, Ash; Graham, Stephen (2010), Cities of Connection and Disconnection, in: Paddison, Ronan; Timberlake, Michael (eds.) (2010), p. 320–356, p. 320, p. 339, p. 419–420. Held, Gerd (2005), Territorium und Großstadt. Die räumliche Differenzierung der Moderne. Wiesbaden. Von Below, Georg (1900), Territorium und Stadt. Aufsätze. Munich, Leipzig.
35 Amin, Ash; Graham, Stephen (1997), The Ordinary City. Transactions of the Institute of British Geographers, p. 420. Amin, Ash; Graham, Stephen (2010), p. 350–355.

5) *Institutions:* The "concentrated and complex institutional base within cities" is often underestimated but plays a huge role in *urban governance*.

Proximity, dense creativity, heterogeneity, functioning as a node, and having an institutional basis – for Amin and Graham, these are the features that make a city a city. Their term for this complex is the *multiplex city*. Currently, theirs is the most modern definition of the city. It allows us to explain and compare phenomena such as a city's function as a *global city* without losing sight of the diversity of *ordinary cities*. The authors do not limit their view to economics, though. While the global city is the prototype of economically successful cities, that is not what one would first assume of ordinary cities if they are to be understood as a counter-project. Amin and Graham, however, believe that the features they identified are prerequisites for economic success. Three conditions are necessary for the latter to be realized:

1) Belonging and trust in *heterogeneity*: The promotion of these two characteristics broadens economic opportunities.
2) *Shared spaces:* Space should not be divided but, as *Richard Sennett* has also noted, different social groups and milieus share the same space.
3) *Openness:* Spatial and social barriers do not permeate the open city. Instead, it avoids *gentrification*, and is not caught in a permanent downward spiral of capital flight, insufficient initiative, and rising costs, together with the threat of criminality, insecurity, and social collapse.

Rather challenging ideas. The method proposed by the authors for achieving this model is no less ambitious. They call it "dialogic" policy that fosters "urban democracy" and "*civic empowerment*".[36] This approach can be applied anywhere, not just to the cities of the Global North. For Amin and Graham, the city is the answer to creating a good life for as many people as possible. A hopeful view that is reminiscent of *Aristotle*. Our next author is likewise interested in the good life.

---

36 Ibid., p. 424–5.

My personal top 10 books

1) Richard Sennett, Building and Dwelling. Ethics for the city, 2018, 394 pages

As stringent and precise as Sennett's arguments are, he never forgets people. The final chapter on Kant and Kantstrasse in Berlin is a masterpiece.

2) Italo Calvino, Invisible Cities, novel, 1978 (original 1972), 176 pages

Fifty-five elegant, visionary portraits with deep insights: "When a man rides a long time through wild regions, he feels the desire for a city." (p. 8)

3) Lewis Mumford, The City in History. Its Origins, Its Transformations, and Its Prospects, 1961, 657 pages

Writer, historian, philosopher, sociologist – Mumford is all of these. His book is wild, audacious, extravagant, and inspiring. "The chief function of the city is to convert power into form, energy into culture, dead matter into the living symbols of art, biological reproduction into social creativity." (p. 571)

4) Roberto Saviano, Gomorrah: A Personal Journey into the Violent International Empire of Naples' Organized Crime System, 2008, Kindle

The author shows what criminality can do to a city based on the example of Naples. Hundreds of murders every year, corruption, violence, and ubiquitous silence. Saviano broke the latter and received death threats because of this book.

5) Stig Dagerman, German Autumn, 2011 (original 1947), 122 pages

In 1947, the Swedish writer travelled through Germany as a reporter for the daily newspaper *Expressen*. His reportages provide an in-depth look at a destroyed land: "These people are Germany's most beautiful ruins, but at the present moment as uninhabitable as the collapsed masses of ruined dwellings... ." (p. 25)

6) Zygmunt Bauman, City of Fears, City of Hopes, 2003, 38 pages

"City dwellers are not necessarily smarter than the rest of humans – but the density of space-occupation results in the concentration of needs. And so questions are asked in the city that were not asked elsewhere, problems arise with which people had no occasion to cope under different conditions." (p. 4–5)

7) Dieter Hoffmann-Axthelm, Die dritte Stadt. Bausteine eines neuen Gründungsvertrages, 1993, 252 pages

After ancient and medieval cities, modern cities are reaching their limits. In future, we will have to negotiate new conditions. As radical and brilliant as its arguments are stringent.

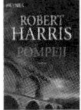

8) Robert Harris, Pompeii: A Novel, 2003, 368 pages

The hours before the volcanic eruption in ancient Pompeii as a gripping mystery written from the perspective of Aquarius, who is responsible for the city's water supply. Harris brings everyday life in the city back to life – and saves the life of his likeable hero.

9) Suketu Mehta, Maximum City: Bombay Lost and Found, 2005, 560 pages

A book that takes you on a journey. Mehta paints a visually stunning picture of the hopes and schemes of Muslim and Hindu gangs. Dark, voluptuous, and rich in description.

10) Dirk Neubauer, Das Problem sind wir, 2019, 234 pages

A breathtaking report about municipal politics. The mayor of the small city of Augustenburg in Saxony exposes a bureaucracy that has forgotten its goals, and tells of active and disillusioned citizens. Eye-opening and encouraging.

55

9. The open city (Richard Sennett)

The sociologist *Richard Sennett* deals with the city in a considerable amount of his work. The essence of his ideas is found in the final instalment of his Homo Faber trilogy, *Building and Dwelling: Ethics for the City*. Sennett is interested in the future: "Should urbanism represent society as it is or seek to change it?"[37] And how can people from diverse backgrounds and with different outlooks live together productively?

To answer these questions, Sennett distinguishes between *ville* and *cité*. For him, the first denotes the city as a whole, the latter a particular place. Ideally, the two fit together seamlessly, but, in reality, the *cité* begins to distinguish itself from the *ville* as a result of growth. Sennett believes the main culprit is the standardization of urban development. "The cities we live in today are closed in ways that mirror what has happened in the tech realm." This leads to the question of the relationship between what is built and what is lived. In a *tour d'horizon*, Sennett analyses past attempts to make cities places where everyone can live well – from *Ildefons Cerdà*'s idea of "fabric", which aimed at equality in *Barcelona* but created monotony, to *Georges-Eugène Baron Haussmann*'s attempt to design *Paris* as a network in order to make the city more accessible, thereby privileging space over place, to *Frederick Law Olmsted*'s Central Park in *New York City*, which promised gregariousness and is in fact built on artificiality. In a nutshell, this analysis led Sennett to be sceptical of master plans that deliver a finished city.

His countermodel is a method for opening cities. First, he looked at the "holy grail of urban design ... to create places which have a particular character." To describe this work, he uses the metaphor of the written word. In texts, an *exclamation mark* is used for extra emphasis, a semicolon breaks the flow that is later ended by a full stop, and *quotation marks* draw attention to a word's meaning or to a statement.

Alongside these urban planning measures, Sennett makes a case for five open forms: 1) The design of public space that is synchronic, where different things can happen at the same time. 2) The creation of porous rather than closed spaces. 3) The conscious but subtle use of markers to call attention to rather unassuming places. 4) The use of type forms that allow for variations and changes. 5) The ability to "plant seeds" and develop various themes while rejecting a city created using a master plan.

---

37   Sennett, Richard (2018), p. 4. The following quotations: p. 211 and p. 241.

Table 4. The text of the city/The city as text

EXCLAMATION MARK !	SEMICOLON ;	"QUOTATION MARKS"
One example is Rome in 1585 under Pope Sixtus V. His aim was to link pilgrimage sites. To this end he erected *obelisks*, which provided orientation and invited pilgrims to go on a spiritual journey. Further examples are *Nelson's Column* in Trafalgar Square, *London*, *La Madelaine* in *Paris*, and numerous equestrian statues.	A *crossing* is a form that breaks the flow. In *New York City*, it gives structure in the form of avenues with stores and offices and residential streets. *Shanghai* and *Barcelona* are similarly structured.	Quotation marks draw attention to where you are. Examples include benches and other street furniture, which do much more than prettify a place.

Richard Sennett's concept of the *open city* is meant to counter groups closing themselves off and is a passionate appeal against thoughtlessness. A great deal of effort is necessary to make "the good life" a little more accessible for many. For Sennett, the most important instrument to this end is a new kind of urban planning: "An open *ville* will avoid committing the sins of repetition and static form; it will create the material conditions in which people might thicken and deepen their experience of collective life." Rather than presenting people with a finished city, Sennett wants to give them the chance to be involved in designing the space they live in.

10. The experts' insights

What, then, do the experts answer when asked: "For which problem is the city a solution?"

- The most radical answer is provided by *Jürgen Friedrichs*: none. That is the consequence of his fundamental refusal to see the city as a separate form.
- *Aristotle* is on the other end of the spectrum. For him, the city has a normative function as a *tool for building the good life*.
- *Werner Sombart* and *Max Weber* give empirical, analytical answers. For Sombart, the city is a structure that organizes diversity, and for Weber it provides the market with a form guaranteed by policy. He deals with heterogeneity by bundling the different kinds of cities into types, thus establishing a method that has consequences to this day.
- *Georg Simmel* and *Lewis Wirth* are interested in interdependencies. Simmel concentrates on *density* and its psychological consequences for the individual. Wirth, in turn, sees the city as a laboratory of society and of modernity. Its main feature is the concentration of heterogeneity. He expanded the structural understanding of the city to include human behaviour and actions.

- In the spirit of Weber, *Saskia Sassen* understands the *global city* as the "command centre" of the global financial economy.
- *Ash Amin* and *Stephen Graham* argue vehemently (with a dash of British humour) against taking a narrow view. For them – and here they concur with *Richard Sennett* – cities are an opportunity to manage diversity. The viewpoints of both Amin and Graham and of Sennett are linked to their basic optimistic trust in human actions, as long as they are buttressed by democratic norms.

As diverse as these proposals are, they all agree on two things: cities organize *density* and *diversity*. Even though each approach makes sense in its own right, there are no criteria for comparing them and measuring their import. We will, therefore, have to try a different approach. It takes us to the word "city" itself, drawing on knowledge from linguistics and linguistic philosophy. It starts with the assumption that, for human beings, language is both a genetic possibility and a cultural reality, so that that which a city means is inscribed in the word for the thing. In the next chapter, we will, therefore, look at the semantic content of the word "city". Currently, the term still seems like a puzzle, in which hiding places are both clear and invisible. "Clear for whoever has found what he was looking for, invisible for whoever does not know that there is something to be sought."[38]

---

38 Ballmann, Bernd (1900), Ein Vexierbild in New York. Kafkas Freiheitsgöttin mit Schwert, in: Harbusch, Ute; Wittkop, Gregor (1900), Kurzer Aufenthalt – Streifzüge durch literarische Orte. Göttingen, p. 271.

C. The wisdom of languages: the city is…

Is there anything hidden in the term "city" that has not already been described, analysed, and interpreted? And could finding it help us fill the gaps that we have identified? *Linguistics* and the *philosophy of language* distinguish between the biological ability to speak and learn languages and language itself. The ability to speak is genetic; language itself is a cultural achievement. That is the foundation of recent findings that "cultural differences are reflected in language in profound ways".[39] Put another way, the meaning of a word is embedded within the word itself. So, anyone who wants to know what the city is must examine the word itself and its meanings.

We do not know how long human beings have been speaking. Our knowledge of written language is on firmer ground. Experts are still debating whether writing first developed in Egypt or in Europe at around 5300 BCE in the *Danube Valley civilization*. It is clear that its cradle was not *Mesopotamia*, a belief long held. We do not know whether there was already a word for "city" at that time. If there was, we can assume that the word tried to express the particularity of this type of settlement.

Today, words for "city" are universal and the meanings associated with them are myriad – changing depending on era, place, and culture. Nevertheless, "a town is always a town wherever it is located in time as well as in space."[40] In the following, we will compare and contrast the words for city in a dozen languages. Together, they are spoken by more than 4.7 billion people. We will begin with the most important languages of antiquity – Egyptian, *Greek*, and *Latin*.

> *Talking about language*
>
> I cannot talk about language without also speaking of the findings of the philologist *Victor Klemperer*. In his 1947 book *LTI Lingua Tertii Imperii* he analyses, as the English title reveals, the Language of the Third Reich. One of his findings was that violence begins with language, in particular the objectification of people. For this reason, I chose not to objectivize or neutralize subjects, including by including all the customary abbreviations, even though others no doubt have noble motives for using them. Respect is more important than efficiency. I have thus sought to use gender-neutral language throughout, knowing full well that it sometimes falls short.

---

39 Deutscher, Guy (2010), Im Spiegel der Sprache. Warum die Welt in anderen Sprachen anders aussieht. Munich, p. 15.
40 Braudel, Fernand (1992), Civilization and Capitalism 15th to 18th Century, Vol. 1: The Structures of Everyday Life, trans. Sian Reynolds. Berkeley, p. 481.

Table 5. World languages

HISTORICAL LANGUAGES					
1) Egyptian	2) Greek	3) Latin			
CONTEMPORARY LANGUAGES	Number of speakers (in millions)				Continent
	Total	Native language	Second language	Countries	
1) Chinese	1,299	n/s	n/s	n/s	Asia
2) English	942	339	603	108	Worldwide
3) Spanish	517	426	91	32	Europe, Latin America
4) Hindi	380	260	120	5	India
5) Arabic	263	n/s	n/s	n/s	Africa
6) French	223	75	153	54	Europe, Africa, Asia
7) Portuguese	208	202	6	12	Europe, Latin America
8) Bengali	208	189	19	5	India
9) Russian	200	171	30	n/s	Europe, Asia
10) German	129	76	52	27	Europe
11) Japanese	128	128	0	3	Asia
12) Korean	77	77	0	8	Asia

In the main, this overview is – like *Werner Sombart*'s seminal essay on the city – based on dictionaries.[41] Sombart limited himself to very few languages – *German, English*, and *French* – that led him to dismiss the method. This is understandable considering the dearth of examples. However, if we include more languages and analyse their terms, the comparability provides a rich field of meanings and also reveals the central core of the concept, which is identical in all languages.

---

41 Sombart, Werner (1931), p. 527–532.

1. The city is dense infrastructure (Egyptian)

Hieroglyphs were in use from around 3200 BCE to about 300 CE. Originally, there were about 700 hieroglyphs, and around 10 times more during the Greek and Roman eras. Hieroglyphs are thus one of the most comprehensive writing systems ever developed.[42] And the hieroglyph for "city" is one of the oldest known terms for it. It is made up of a circle with a diagonal cross in the centre. From it, we can deduce that the Egyptian understanding of the city was very formal. The city is separated from its environment and forms its own *unit*, divided into sections by a street crossing. What it is separating itself from is not defined. Perhaps it had its own status, or even a certain measure of *autonomy* and its own law. That would certainly fit logically with this form. We cannot know from this sign whether or not this unit is connected to other units.

Figure 5. Egyptian hieroglyph for "city".

We can, however, understand it as marking the city as a *dense* space that allows for *diversity*, since the quarters could stand for different functions. But the hieroglyph says the most about *infrastructure*. Streets are the most important element of the urban fabric and are never more clearly embedded in any other term for the city than they are here. The Egyptian hieroglyph thus describes a structural concept of the city. It sees the city as a separate form with its own logic, one that could be described as *dense infrastructure*.

2. The city is citizenship (Greek)

Some of the most important ideas about the city were developed in the language of *Aristotle* and *Plato*, of *Sophocles* and *Demosthenes* – classical Greek or, more precisely, the Attic dialect. They retain their importance to this day, although now only the core settlement of the *polis* of antiquity is thought of as a "city". Originally, *"polis"* meant a fortified hilltop settlement. In *Athens* up until the late 5th century, the term was synonymous with the *Acropolis*. Features of a *polis* are a certain *number* of inhabitants and buildings, as well a number of institutions that, in turn, constitute the city as a *unit*.

The classical Greek understanding has two particularities. One element is its central function *in* and *for* a larger area. At the *polis*, the core urban settlement is connected to the surrounding area to become a unit. It can function as a hub for a) political management and steering, b) sacral life, or c) the economy (market). This functional view makes the term fuzzy, though, because the Greek *polis* can mean both "city" and "state" *(POLITEIA, ΠΟΛΙΤΕΙΑ)*.

---

42 Schenkel, Wolfgang (1997), Tübinger Einführung in die klassisch-ägyptische Sprache und Schrift. Tübingen. aaew.bbaw.de/tla/servlet/S05?d=d001&h=h001 (accessed: 23 Apr. 2022).

> **ⓘ** *One of the best descriptions of the polis*
>
> "The p. is a collective and responsible association that is able to make binding decisions internally and act in concert externally. Its order is based on the rule of law. The p. is protected by a deity that ensures its continuation; community rituals are constitutive for the p. The members of the association, the citizens, who also make up its military potential, are the constitutive elements of the community, not the physical city or its walls. The p. is threatened by stasis and any division among the citizens, up to and including civil war. For its continuation, the p. therefore needs citizens to accept responsibility and foster friendship and harmony (*homonoia*). The more citizens are seen as active subjects, the more autarchy and oligarchy become incompatible with the essence of the p.; the internal self-government of the citizenry (which implies equality) and external autonomy are the preferred requirements of freedom. External features include the *agora*, the *prytaneion* (site of the central hearth), the *bouleuterion*, the *gymnasium*, and the temple; the governmental unit can be seen in the existence of only one *prytaneion* and *bouleuterion*."[43]

The second particularity is the *polis*'s function as the community of the *politai*, the citizens. This is a new and epochal definition. It was developed over a long period of time and can be understood as a response to external threats and to a crisis of leadership in archaic times. In the *polis*, responsibility is no longer centralized, but distributed across many, thus limiting how much power one person can wield and for how long. This remains one of the central tenets of democracy. Its main feature is the *politeuma* (*ΠΟΛΙΤΕΥΜΑ*), the special new form of government. What is also new is the concept of the citizen (ΠΟΛΙΤΗΣ) and his involvement in and identification with the community.

And so the *polis* for the first time established an urban community of citizens. That is its relevance, even though the urban inhabitants who were elevated to the status of citizenry only made up a small (and exclusively male) portion of the population. Nevertheless, this represented an innovative paradigm shift for the city. From then on, it was no longer solely the *object* of or *platform* for royal rule, but was able to act independently as a *subject*. The *polis* became a blueprint for a new form of living together. That had two consequences, one whose impact was mostly internal and one that was more important for the outside world.

a) The greatest influence the *polis* brought to bear was that it established an association of citizens. This function allowed even small settlements to become cities, although they would not be considered such by the size of their population. What is key is the transformation from inhabitant to citizen, which led to a separation of the public and private spheres. In public, citizens take on responsibility and are given the opportunity to act politically. This initi-

---

43 Nippel, Wilfried (1989), Polis, in: Ritter, Joachim; Gründer, Karlfried (1989), Historisches Wörterbuch der Philosophie. Bd. 7: P–Q. Darmstadt, S. 1032.

ated a process that made it necessary to keep renegotiating the rights and duties of the citizen.
b) To see the *polis* as its own organizational form also means understanding it as holding *autonomy* or being willing and able to shape its own life.[44]

As *Aristotle* summed it up, the mission of the city is to provide its citizens with the ability to allow them to live a good and moral life. In antiquity, it became a tool to help people to live a "better" life. This was also a response to the question of how to get away from the crises that resulted from the despotic rule of royals. To this day, the *polis* remains one of the most sophisticated concepts of the city. Thanks to *Ancient Greece*, we have a model of rule that continues to be relevant: the urban society of citizens.

3. The city is power politics (Latin)

The Roman Empire was an urban culture. One of its most characteristic instruments of dominance, which was key to its culture, was a system of different types of cities. Latin therefore has many words for the city, the most important being *oppidum, urbs, municipium, colonia,* and *civitas*. Each stands for certain tasks; together they form a nuanced system of cities.

The centre was *Urbs Roma*, the capital and centre; the other types made up the periphery. In Latin, instead of the long catalogues of features found in almost all other languages, we find only certain infrastructural elements like the city wall and the underlining of the importance of the citizen and his rights and duties. Noticeable in comparison to the *polis* is that in both cases the understanding of the city is explicitly political. A new type of rule is at the centre of the *polis*, with its urban society of citizens. This seems to have at first been true of the *civitas*, but that changed at the latest when Rome turned from a republic into an empire. The urban society of citizens became a society of power; the emperors at the top managed an imperium and had their own lifestyle.

---

44 Mann, Christian (2010), Politische Partizipation und die Vorstellung des Menschen als Zoon Politikon, in: Hansen, Mogens Herman (ed.) (2010), Démocratie Athénnien – Democratie Moderne: Tradition et Influences. Geneva, p. 51–65.

> ℹ️ *Roman terms for the city*
>
> *Oppidum:* The most common Latin term for the city originally denoted a tribe's castle, or a suburb or district of a civitas fortified by a wall. The *oppidum*, verifiable since the 7th century BCE, became a city through the "concentration of the population and social differentiation". The city wall, which guarantees security, is its most important feature. *Oppidum* literally means "fortified place" and is usually used to denote smaller cities, in the main *rural towns*, sometimes also as a synonym for *urbs*, the most important denotation for Rome (Livius: 42.20.3). The term is used for settlements both within and without the empire. It is the only one of the five most important Latin terms for the city that says nothing about the legal status of the settlement.
>
> *Urbs:* "In the broadest sense, u. denotes a large city geographically and politically, or more narrowly (since *Sallust* and *Cicero*), the capitol Rome, the symbol of Roman 'urbanity'." To distinguish it from *oppidum*, *urbs* was usually understood (when not referring to the city of Rome) as a large city, usually without walls, with its own legal status. The word's root appears early on in other Latin terms, such as *urbanitas*, which means "politeness", "finesse", and "good education". Hence the term refers to a specific urban lifestyle.
>
> *Municipium:* This term denotes duties and achievements. It is also linked to the verb *capere* (to take, accept, take hold, occupy). Originally used for *rural areas* that were not Roman, from *Caesar's* reign it was also applied to the provinces. Those peoples whose land was annexed by the Romans were brought into their empire as *socii* (confederates). Their cities (*municipia*) remained autonomous in terms of administration and civil law, but their inhabitants had to serve in the Roman military. "One after the other, the municipia received gradations of civil rights and participated in various forms in Roman constitutional life." *Municipium* hence denotes a legal status in relation to Rome.
>
> *Colonia:* "colony", "settlement", and "town" are the main meanings of the word *colonia*, which is linked to the verb *colere*, "to cultivate" or "to inhabit". "During the expansion of Roman rule, in large parts of Italy founding colonies was the instrument used to secure [Roman] power." Therefore, Roman colonies were "new municipalities with Roman citizens who administered themselves but retained full civil rights." Politically, this describes a dependency on Rome, although a *colonia* held more extensive rights than an *oppidum*.
>
> *Civitas:* The most important Latin word for city means "citizenry", "civil rights", "community", "nation", "urban community", and "city". *Civitas* is the community of citizens – to some extent comparable to the *polis*. "The Romans used the term mainly for foreign communities, while Roman citizens as a whole were referred to as *populus Romanus* or 'the Roman people'." Civitas thus mainly denotes the specifically Roman city-state, that form of government that is based on an urban society of citizens.

Rome as the centre of power defined a concept that has often served as a role model. In this model, the Roman system of city-states is a driver for garnering and preserving power. Accordingly, the Latin terms for "city" deliver the first nuanced, functional typology of the city that marks it out as the core element of Roman rule.

4. The city is structured densification (Spanish)

The Spanish word for the city, *ciudad*, *stems from* the Latin word *civitas*. Despite this linguistic proximity, citizens are not part of the explicit content of the term. The Spanish understanding of the word is more formal. *Ciudad* is defined as "the entirety of buildings and streets under the direction of a *municipal administration*. It has a high population *density* and numerous inhabitants are, as a rule, employed in *non-agricultural sectors*".[45]

The citizen that is still present in the Latin root is replaced by the size and density of the population. The naming of both is worthy of note, for it underlines not only a numerical but also a qualitative component of this feature.

What is also striking is the economic dimension of the Spanish understanding of the city. It stresses that most of the population does not do agricultural work. This references the characteristic division of labour and *diversity* within the city that differentiates it from the countryside.

The term used to denote cities and urban areas of transregional importance is *ciudad capitalina*. However, it is not precise enough, since in practice it is used for almost every administrative unit that enjoys a certain *autonomy*.

Spanish also has the terms *núcleo poblacional* (population centre), *conjunto urbano* (urban complex), and *área metropolitana* (metropolitan area) that are comprised of the terms included in the semantic content of *ciudad*, that is *población*, *metrópoli*, and *urbe*. The term *metrópoli*, which has its roots in the Latin *metropolis*, which in turn stems from the Greek μητρόπολις, has the Spanish meanings: 1) capital city, administrative seat of the province or state, 2) archdiocese that has suffragan bishops under it, 3) nation and original city in reference to its colonies. Another Spanish term for city is *urbe*, which is used for large cities and rooted in the Latin *urbs*.

As a rule, the Spanish terms for city are formal. The Latin meaning of a society of citizens is still present in *ciudad*. *Density* and *structure* are key semantic content, whereby the former refers to the population and the latter to the political administration and look of the city. All in all, the Spanish terms for "city" are not very nuanced. To differentiate between different types of cities and varying functions, additional terms are needed. In sum, "city" in Spanish can be understood as *structured densification*.

---

45 Corominas, Joan; Pascual, José A. (1991–1997, followed by several new editions; the 2001 edition is cited here), Diccionario etimologico castellano e hispánico, Vol. 2: Ce–f. Madrid, p. 153.

5. The city is lifestyle (French)

Ville is the French word for "city". It stems from the Latin *villa* and originally meant agricultural cultivation. In the Middle Ages, *ville* was used to denote settlements, mostly fortified ones.

To distinguish further, the French uses a complement. Well into the 19th century, the *ville forte* or *ville fortifiée*, a mid-size city surrounded by ramparts or walls, was the most characteristic form of city. This has led to a variety of denotations for the city that are oriented towards population size. *Village* is a village, a *petite ville* is a *small city*, and a *grande ville* a *large city*. A similar denotation is used for other city types, for example a *vielle ville* (old city) or *satellite ville* (satellite city* or suburb).

The *ville* is defined as "a geographical and social milieu formed by a relatively large agglomerate of buildings and, importantly, inhabitants".[46] The division of labour is also important, for these inhabitants should "in the main work within this agglomerate in the areas of trade, industry, and administration." The *ville*, in contrast to *Richard Sennett's* cherished *cité*, which denotes only the city centre or residential area, is comprised of the city as a whole.

The word acquired a further meaning in the modern era. In the 17th century, *la ville* – in contrast to the countryside – became a synonym for the sophisticated and intellectual social life of *Paris*. The emphasis on the urban lifestyle within the French concept of the city is equalled only, if it all, by the *Japanese*. This understanding of the concept is found in numerous, often charming, sayings.

All in all, the French concept of the city encompasses both quantitative – i.e. size, number of buildings and inhabitants, and thus also *density* – and qualitative meanings. This includes structural political and economic aspects, in particular the non-agricultural character of the urban economy with its division of labour. There is also great emphasis, that is on the urban lifestyle, the great innovation of the French concept of the city.

Table 6. French sayings

---

dîner en ville: (*dîner* = to eat dinner) to eat out, to be invited to dinner

baise-en-ville: (*baiser* = a kiss, to kiss) a small overnight bag

villes et filles qui parlementent sont à moitié rendues: "Cities and girls that negotiate, have already half surrendered."

---

[46] Dictionnaire de la langue française. Le Grand Robert (1985), Vol. IX. Paris, p. 746. The following quotations: ibid, p. 746.

6. The city is relevance (English)

According to Webster's New Encyclopedic Dictionary "*city*" is defined (at least in American English) as "an inhabited place of greater size or importance than a town".[47] Unlike in French, *size* and *relevance* are accentuated.

On the one hand, the English concept is quantitative and comparative. It is population size that distinguishes a *city* from a *town*. Although the terms are often used interchangeably, a town is "larger than a village, but smaller than a city". Size (population) and the corresponding *density* as well as the differentiation from a rural settlement (*village*) are the main features of the *city*.

On the other hand, relevance is a key feature of the English term. This is partly dictated by size, but not only by size. Hence, *city* also stands for a historical place with a bishop's see and a cathedral, as well as for a city with a royal charter and ceremonial privileges. These features emphasize the city's function and the importance it gained in history as a political and religious centre.

Further, the *city* is often used internationally by both urban researchers and on the street to mean the city centre. That use has its roots in the development of *London*, where in the 18th century the *City of London* was first used to denote the financial district while other functions were concentrated in other parts of the city, for example the government in the *City of Westminster*.

The main meanings of the word "city" in English are size, status, and function. It is used not only quantitatively but also denotes a place's status, the second feature. The third feature, namely function, qualifies the meaning. There are no further meanings in English. Reference is only indirectly made to a many-tiered economy or to lifestyle. The English concept of the city is formal and lacking in content. It therefore lends itself easily to additional, qualifying terms. That explains the popularity of new concepts of the city that have come out of English-speaking countries, of which the *global city* and the *smart city* are currently the best known.

Table 7. Features of the city in English

- Spatial division into functional districts
- Nuanced development
- Decrease in residential population since the development of modern cities
- High density of workplaces
- Larger population by day than by night
- Low percentage of manufacturing industry
- High land prices and rents
- External characteristics (store windows, density of buildings, representational value)

---

47   Webster's New Encyclopedic Dictionary (1993). New York City, p. 179.

7. The city is rights (German)

The *Duden*, the standard German dictionary, defined *Stadt* in the 1980s as "a larger closed settlement that enjoys certain rights and represents the administrative, economic, and cultural centre of a region".[48] This definition was expanded in 2001, in one of the last printed editions, to specify that a city is also a "large cluster of houses (also public buildings) in which many people live in one administrative area".

Other dictionaries name the same features, defining *Stadt* almost identically as a "large, closed settlement that makes up an economic and cultural centre". Four features characterize the city in German: a) *size* (many people, large number of houses, distinguishing between private and public), which includes *densification*; b) the *enclosure* or *unity* of the settlement; c) its function as a *hub*; and d) a catalogue of *rights*.

The importance of *municipal law* in German, which is not pinpointed in the same way in any other language, can be traced back to the Middle Ages. The German word for *Stadt* comes from the Old High German *stat*, meaning "place", which from the 12th century denoted a locality or settlement. These were defined by their status and their privileges such as market rights (*Marktrecht*) or minting privileges (*Münzrecht*).

In their *Deutsches Wörterbuch* (German Dictionary), *Jacob* and *Wilhelm Grimm* further referenced the difference between Low High German *statt*, or *stete*, and Middle High German *stätte*, noting that the spelling of *Stadt* was for a long time "merely an orthographic means of differentiating from '*statt*' or '*instead*'". "The development of the meaning of our word," the Grimms' dictionary continues, "was not least helped along by the common juxtaposition of castle and city".[49]

For a long time, the German term for "city" (*Stadt*) rivalled the term "castle" (*Burg*). This link mirrors the medieval view of the city, differentiates it from the village and also references *antiquity*. In the Middle Ages, the city represented security, one of the oldest and highest values in an environment that was often hostile. Not until the late Middle Ages did the semantic content of the terms diverge and did the *city* supersede the *castle* – semantically and in reality.

In sum, the German concept of the city combines the main quantitative features of *size* (population) and *density* with varying functions and issues. The main functions are *central function* and *unity*; the most important issues are *administration*, the *economy, culture*, and *rights*. The concept of the citizen that is so central to the Greek *polis* and also, though to a lesser degree, the Latin *civitas* (and present merely as a formality in the Spanish *ciudad*) is lacking in German, as it is in English and French. While the French emphasizes lifestyle and the English relevance, in German the key feature of the city is its legal status.

---

48 Duden, Bedeutungswörterbuch (1985). Mannheim, Leipzig, Vienna, Zurich, p. 605.
49 Grimm, Jacob; Grimm, Wilhelm (2004, original 1854–1960), Deutsches Wörterbuch. Digital version of the first edition. Frankfurt a. M. Vol. 10.2.1; stabgold – stählen Vol. 10.2.1, p. 1906.

My personal top 10 urban music

1) John Lennon, Walls & Bridges, 1974

The darkest highlight of the 1970s. Lennon's voice is more clear-cut and piercing on this album than ever before or since. New York City – *Steel and glass, steel and glass – Mm, mm, mm, mm.*

2) George Gershwin, Rhapsody in Blue, 1924

"How trite and feeble and conventional … how sentimental and vapid the harmonic treatment. … Weep over the lifelessness of the melody and harmony, so derivative, so stale, so inexpressive."[50] Lawrence Gilman in the *New York Tribune*, 1924. Is it possible to be more wrong?

3) Grandbrothers, Open, 2017

Warm and electronic, rigid and playful, intellectual and emotional, atonal and rhythmic. The sound enters your ears and takes root in your head and guts. State-of-the-art urban sound and vision.

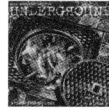

4) Goran Bregović, Underground, 1995

Country or city? Folk or punk? Secular or sacral? Or everything at once? As crazy as the Balkan states' search for identity. No cliché is left out, yet it's all as authentic as humanly possible. Crying – Laughing – Bregović.

5) Buena Vista Social Club, 1997

"One day, out of the blue, there was a knock on my door. – What are you doing? – I'm just shining my shoes. – I've been looking for you, come with me. – I told him I don't want to sing any more. But he said 'No, man, I need you' So I ask him when, Tomorrow? I said. And he said 'No, right now' … All I had time for was to wash my face and wipe the shoe polish off my hands. So we came here, to the Egrem studios." *Ibrahim Ferrer*

6) Bob Marley, Burnin', 1973

Fast, danceable ska, radically understated folk music (with African elements) … words cannot describe the magic of reggae so magical, not even Eric Clapton stands a chance. Sound invented in the slums of Kingston: desperate, passionate, and full of hope.

7) Ideal, Ideal, 1980

Rebellious, female and very, very West Berlin. "Oranienstraße, where the Quran lives | down the street the wall begins | Mariannenplatz where red is in | I feel good, I'm into Berlin!"

8) The Clash, London Calling, 1979

War, hunger, floods, nuclear meltdowns: Joe Stummer and Mick Jones's cry for help – an eminently danceable dystopian hymn.

9) David Bowie, Heros, 1977

"[The Studio] is about thirty or forty metres away from the wall … and there's a tower right on top … every day during the lunch break a boy and a girl would meet under the wall, under the guard, under the gun, on a park bench. … They were carrying on some kind of affair. … And it struck me as ironic that out of all the hundreds of places they could have met in West Berlin they met under the wall." *David Bowie*

10) Psy, Gangnam Style, 2012

"Big brother in Gangnam style!" The singer Psy satirizes the luxury lifestyle in the wealthy Gangnam neighbourhood and people's attempts to imitate it. The most frequently viewed YouTube video to date with over 3.5 billion klicks in less than 10 years.

---

50 Cited in Slonimsky, Nicolas (2000, original 1953), Lexicon of Musical Invective. New York, p. 105.

8. The city is the centre (Russian)

The Russian word город (gorod) has two main meanings: *size* and *hub,* or *centre*.[51] To qualify as a city, a place must have at least 12,000 inhabitants, and 85 per cent of them must *not* work in agriculture. Having a central function means that it is the hub of an *oblast,* or district, as regards trade, industry, culture, and politics.

The *capital city* functions as the hub of a country. Its status is linked to power and the provision of security, which until the 19th century was expressed by means of a *city wall*, an element used around the globe to separate inside from outside. Many etymologically related words from the Slavic languages refer to this function of the city as a hub. In eastern Slavic countries, the first cities were fortified settlements, and the term город means "fenced-in space". "The medieval city in Russia was a fortified area, surrounded by a wall, which distinguished it from a village."[52] Thus, formally, the city is a fortified settlement. The wall not only separates the city from the surrounding area, it also defines it as a *unit* with an inner structure. Usually, old Russian cities were made up of a centre, the *kremlin*, and the outer city, the *posad*, where the tradespeople and traders worked and lived.

In a nutshell, the most prominent meaning of the Russian term for "city" is its function as a *centre* or *hub* – not surprisingly considering the size of the country. Also key to the Russian concept is *size* – whereby in Russia (as in Japan) the number of inhabitants needed to call a place a city is relatively high in an international comparison – as well as a population with non-agrarian livelihoods and a clear division of labour into *politics* (administration), *economics* (industry and trade), and *culture*.

9. The city is civilization (Arabic)

مدينة | madina is derived from the word for civilization, ة المدنيّ, and means "people congregated in a centralized, delimited settlement with roads that is outside of the desert and has its own administrative structure and supply system".

There are two Arabic words for civilization: *al-hadara* and *al-madaniyya*. *Al-hadara* denotes a sedentary – as opposed to nomadic – population. *Al-madaniyya*, in turn, stems from *madina*, or city. There is a third, *medieval*, term for civilization: *al-umran*.

In this case, too, there is a direct connection to the city, for the word means "to populate, to build, to construct, to be populated, to be cultured".[53] The opposites "city" and "countryside", "sedentary" and "nomadic" are prominent in the

---

51 Bol'šaja Sovetskaja Ènciklopedija (1969–1978). Moscow, 30 vols.
52 Tichomirov, Mikhail Nikolaevich (1956), Mittelalterliche russische Städte. "Drevnerusskie gorod". 2nd revised and completed edition. Moscow.
53 Schregle, Götz (1999), Wörterbuch Deutsch-Arabisch. Wiesbaden, p. 1126–1127.

Arabic concept of the city. Taken to the extreme, this dualism can be expressed in the formula: city = civilization; countryside = desert. The Arabic term for "city" entails five main meanings:

1) *Size:* There is no exact numeric definition of a "congregation" of people, rather size is defined in relation to other units. مدينة (*madina*), plural مدن = city, cities; بلدة (*balada*), plural; بلاد = place, village, *town*, or their respective plurals; بلد (*balad*), plural بلدان, = place, country, state and places, countries, states, respectively.
2) *Structures:* The understanding of structure in the Arabic concept of the city refers to the administration and political functions as well as to infrastructure.
3) *Unit:* The delimitation of the city marks it as a unit.
4) *Centre:* Its function as a hub is linked to the city's qualification as a unit.
5) *Civilization:* The fifth meaning is the most remarkable. It is reminiscent of similar content in Latin, French, and Japanese.

> ⓘ The Islamic city
>
> The word for "city" holds special meaning in the Islamic world owing to the eponymous city المدينة المنوّرة (*al-Madīna al-munawwarah*) in modern-day Saudi Arabia. It is the second-most holy place after Mecca, the birthplace of the prophet Mohammed. Literally, medina means "illuminated city" or "city of lights".
>
> This term honours the prophet's migration (هجرة/*higira*) from Mecca to Medina in 622 CE, the beginning of the Islamic calendar. In the following years, Islam spreads throughout the Arabic countries, building on the Hellenistic–Roman tradition that had taken root there earlier and replacing it with a new structure. In the east and west in particular, new cities arose in the conquered areas including *Kairouan, Rabat, Fez,* and *Cairo,* and later a chain of cities that led from Spain (*Córdoba*) across northern Africa, the Near East and Central Asia all the way to India.
>
> In the 10th and 11th centuries, the large cities in the Islamic countries were the most populated places in the western hemisphere. *Baghdad* and *Cairo* alone, with over a quarter of a million inhabitants, were among the largest cities in the world at the time. *Aleppo, Damascus,* and *Tunis* also boasted respectable populations of between 50,000 and 100,000.

In sum, a "city" in Arabic is a large, structured unit; an achievement of civilization. This is reminiscent of *Aristotle*'s view of the city as a way of enabling a good life.

10. The city is prosperity (Hindi)

Since taking the diversity of languages on the Indian continent into account is beyond the scope of this overview, the following concentrates on one of India's most important languages, namely Hindi. *Nagar* and *shahar* both mean "city" in this language and denote an area that has been settled, whereby the "number of inhabitants has grown ... and become wealthier".⁵⁴ This definition names three features: *population size, growth,* and *prosperity.* The implicit reference to *size* (population) in connection with growth is important. This reflects a theory of development, whereby a village becomes a city. This thesis is centred around the opportunity to increase wealth. Here, too, the city is a tool. The formula would be: city = prosperity.

Table 8. Hindi terms for "city"

NAGAR	SHAHAR	MAHANAGAR
...(fem.: *nigari*) has a Sanskrit root and is used in the Indian epos *Mahabharata* to denote a city. The book mentions the capital city *Viratnagar* (now *Bairat*). To underline size and importance, *nagar* is often given the prefix *maha* (महा; large, imposing, important, prominent, honourable). As in English, "city" is linked to importance, as in an important place.	...is the Persian word for city, and is a synonym for *nagar* and *pur.* The many Persian words in *Hindi* and *Urdu* are a result of the three-centuries-long presence of the *Mughal Empire* (1526–1858) on the continent of India, where the official language was Persian.	...means strong, large, and important city (*metropolis*). Alongside size (and, implictly, *diversity*) the other key feature, powerful, puts political connotations at the fore. The word *rajdhani*, derived from Sanskrit, means "seat of the royal house". The capital (*rajdhani*) was historically always the place where the king or ruler (*raj*) had his residence (*dhani*).

In sum, the Indian term characterizes the city as a tool for prosperity. Hence, economic importance is underlined, as is size (relevance) and proximity to the ruler.

11. The city is the economy (Chinese)

Chéng shì 城市, the *Mandarin* word for "city", means a "densely settled area where industry and business are highly developed".⁵⁵ This makes *size* and economic *function* the key features. To better understand these meanings we must take a closer look at the ideograph. *Chéng shi* is a two-syllable word. The first syllable is a *huiyi* or compound character, 城 (*chéng*), that draws its meaning from the ideograph. The part on the left, (土), means earth, the part on

---

54 Vidal, Denis; Gupta, Narayani (1999), Northern India, City Words. Working Paper No. 4. Urban vocabulary in Northern India. UNESCO. Gatzlaff-Hälsig, Margot (1993), Grammatischer Leitfaden des Hindi. Leipzig, Berlin, Munich, Vienna, Zurich, New York, p. 684. Sharma, Aryendra; Vermeer, Hans J. (1987), Hindi-Deutsches Wörterbuch. Heidelberg, p. 935, p. 1292, p. 1435, and p. 1537.. Monier-Williams, Monier; Cappeller, Carl; Leumann, Ernst (2005), Sanskrit-English dictionary. Etymologically and philologically arranged with special reference to cognate indo-european languages. New ed. greatly enl. and impr. Giessen, New Delhi, Chennai, p. 525.
55 Deutsch-Chinesisches Wörterbuch (1983), Shanghai. Cíyuán (1995, 6th ed., original 1988), Shanghai, p. 326. Cíhǎi, (1985, 5th ed., original 1980), Shanghai, p. 346.

the right determines the pronunciation. Originally, the character meant *city wall*. In China there is, as a rule, a two-tiered system, in which the inner wall is called 城 *(chéng)* and the outer wall 郭 *(guo)*. These walls typically delimited the *imperial capital*, private property, and royal fiefdoms. The walls also draw a boundary between the city and the countryside. While the city walls now usually remain open or, as in *Beijing*, remain only as historical attractions, the principle of inclusion and exclusion still plays a major role in Chinese cities.

The characters 城 *(chéng)* and 市 *(shì)* are used to denote places in which many people live together. Originally, *shì* stood for a market. Places in which people do business and live together later become residential centres, from which the meaning of "city" in Chinese is derived. As in Hindi, this suggests a development through which a village becomes a city. In modern Mandarin, there is hardly any difference any more between *chéng* and *shì*. Either ideogram can be added to the name of a city, for example. The meaning is the same. For instance, Chinese people call the city of *Berlin* either 柏林城 *(bólín chéng)* or 柏林市 *(bólín shì)*.

The size of a city is exactly defined in Mandarin. A distinction is drawn between small, mid-size, large cities, and megacities, whereby a small European city already qualifies as a *large city*.

In a nutshell, the Chinese term for "city" is characterized by its emphasis on the importance of the economy. Size and density are also key features. As in Japanese, a distinction is made between small, mid-size, and large cities, and megacities.

> **ⓘ** *The urbanization of China*
>
> The urbanization of China is progressing more rapidly than in any other country. In 1980, China was still steeped in its agricultural tradition, and only 20 per cent of the population lived in cities. Twenty years later, that percentage had doubled; by 2012, 52.6 per cent of the population were living in an urban area.
>
> In March 2016, the Chinese Premier, Li Keqiang, declared the continuation of planned urbanization to be one of the government's most important objectives. By 2025, 250 million more people are to be relocated to cities, raising the urban population to 70 per cent, or over 900 million individuals.
>
> Urbanization has never before progressed on such a scale on our planet. The government's reason for this push is to increase and accelerate value creation and economic growth.

Table 9. How Mandarin differentiates between the size of a city

小城市	中小城市	大城市	特大城市
xiao chéng shì	zhong xiao chéng shì	da chéng shì	te da chéng shì
Small cities	Mid-size cities	Large cities	Megacities
pop. < 200,000	pop. 200,00–500,000	pop. 500,000–1m	pop. > 1m

12. The city is a hub (Japanese)

都市 (*toshi*) is the Japanese word for "city". It is defined as an "identifiable geographical population centre with political, economic, and cultural structures at its core". The Japanese social sciences define the term in a similar way: "Within the national community, *toshi* is understood to mean those settlements that feature social hubs such as administrative institutions, schools, stores, and offices, and are delimited from the unit of the village (*sonraku* | 村落)."[56] The term *toshi* has its etymological origins in the *kanji* (characters) for *to* (都) and *shi* (市).

Table 10. Japanese terms for "city"

to (都) on its own means:	shi (市) on its own means:
- The seat of government; - The place where the emperor lives, permanently or temporarily; - A place with many inhabitants; - An administrative unit (e.g. 東京都 = Tokyo = capital city Tokyo) – which includes and qualifies the term "unit"; - Elegant (presumably because the emperor lived there); - To govern, to control; - Everyone, everything. Historically, kanji 都 also denotes the site of the former monarch's mausoleum, as well as the site at which people gather together because that is where the mausoleum is.	- A place where goods are traded; - A place where people and things gather; - A shopping street; - Public administrative bodies as defined by the Act on Local Autonomy (地方自治法/*Chihô Jichi-Hô*), which applies to settlements that fulfil three criteria: • A pop. of at least 50,000; • At least 60 per cent of the land is built up with residential buildings; • At least 60 per cent of inhabitants work in trade and industry.

Size and *density* are precisely defined for a Japanese city: it must have at least 50,000 inhabitants at least 60 per cent of whom work in industry and commerce (and hence not in agriculture), and residential buildings must cover at least 60 per cent of its area. These numbers allow for a clear differentiation between cities and suburbs, industrial areas, or very large villages. This definition makes the Japanese term for "city" one of the most precise. There are more features besides size. A city must also have a public administration, which implies a certain level of *autonomy*. Furthermore, *diversity* or a mixture of functions is necessary.

Thus, in Japanese "city" means the nuanced interaction of people and structures. It is derived from various functions of *politics* (seat of government and administration, imperial residence), the *economy* (production, commerce, shopping streets, neighbourhoods, and districts), and *culture* (preserving the heritage of the past, mausoleum, celebrating festivals).

The Japanese concept of the city is remarkable for its ambiguity and its precision, as well as the emphasis on an urban lifestyle, which is otherwise speci-

---

56   Kojien No. 4/Shinmura (1991), Tokyo, p. 1846 and p. 2474; Kurasawa, Susumu (1985), Die japanische Sozialwissenschaft, Vol. 7. Die Stadt, Chapter 8: Einführungsaufsatz zum städtischen Lebensstil. Tokyo, p. 96.

fied so clearly only in Latin and French. This distinguishes it from, for example, Russian, which also underlines the city's function as a centre, but in the sense of power politics and management.

13. The genes of the city

Around 20 academic fields, nine experts, and a dozen languages – what image emerges from their analysis? The meaning of the word "city" in 12 languages reveals a diversity of content, and the results of the research done by experts and within academic fields are just as broad and varied. The differences between languages have regional and cultural roots. Yet they are neither arbitrary nor meaningless, and reveal more than the results that have been summarized so far in this book.[57] The meanings inherent in each of the respective languages reveal at least five common features. Four of these are found in all languages and describe the city as a structure. This special structure can be distinguished from others and creates the framework within which people act. Let us look more closely at its features.

Size, density, densification

Size is an integral part of most concepts of the city, and is often highlighted in semantic content, in academic fields, and by all the experts. *Aristotle* is an exception. He emphasizes function and assumes a larger settlement. *Latin* and *French* also do not explicitly mention size, but assume it as a given.

As a rule, size refers to the number of inhabitants. In *Russian*, *Chinese*, and *Japanese*, that number is even quantified. Russian and Japanese are both interesting in that they name a lower limit. Occasionally, size also refers to space or area, or to an unspecified but large number of buildings. Population and space together point towards a core definition of the city, that is *density*. In *Spanish*, *German*, Chinese, and Japanese it forms an express part of semantic content, and German is particularly precise by emphasizing *densification* and not merely describing a moment in time. In sum: *the city is densification*.

Diversity and heterogeneity

Diversity is the second feature that the comparison highlights. It can be inferred from the context in all languages, and is explicitly named in *French*. It refers in the main to the diversity of the working population as opposed to its rural counterpart and is thus a functional and social concept. This feature of the city is also named in all academic disciplines and by all researchers and philosophers. Bringing the two top features together, we can define the city as *heterogeneous densification*.

---

57   Prell, Uwe (2016), Theorie der Stadt in der Moderne. Kreative Verdichtung. Opladen, Berlin, Toronto, p. 40–111.

Unity

The city is a *unit* – that is the third feature. It is named in almost all languages, it is only in *English* and *Hindi* that it is inferred from other features. While this characteristic is also underlined in all disciplines, not all the experts emphasize it. For some, it plays no role or is simply assumed as a given. *Jürgen Friedrich*'s theory can even be read as a counterargument. In numerous languages the term is rendered more precisely and usually defined politically as an *administrative unit*, for example in *Greek, Latin, Spanish, German, Russian, Chinese, Japanese*, and *Arabic*. The city is, thus, a political, geographical, economic, or social structure that is delimited from other units. In political science and sociology, the city can also be understood as an institution, making it comparable with other *institutions*. No matter which perspective one prefers, the concepts of *status* and *relevance* are linked to the word "unit", in particular in *English* and *German*, but also in *Hindi*. The city is, therefore, a *unit* with its own (*legal*) *status* and *relevance*. Bringing these three features together, the city is a *densified, heterogeneous unit*.

Structure

The fourth feature is found in the semantic content of all of the languages studied, in all academic disciplines, and is also named by all the experts. But the meaning of this very open concept can only be pinned down by its use. If, for example, the city is seen as an *administrative unit*, that assumes a network of horizontal and vertical political structures. If the city's function as a *hub* or *centre* is referenced, the emphasis is on its relationship to the surrounding area. Both of these meanings are still abstract. The term "structure" is easier to understand when it refers to *infrastructure* and to individual elements, such as a *city wall*, *streets*, or *squares*. If we bring all four of the above-named meanings together, the city is a *densified, heterogeneous, structured unit*. What have we learned so far?

Conditions for acting within the city

Densification, diversity, unity, and *structure* – taken separately, none of these terms is sufficient to clearly delineate the city. A large unit is not necessarily a city. A refugee camp can also be a densified unit. It is possible to test all the possible combinations following the above pattern – none of them delivers a meaningful definition, because none of them specifies what is typical of a city. The four terms do, however, provide a clearly defined framework. If we understand the city as a densified, heterogeneous, structured unit, we have defined the framework within which people act. That is true for the actions of individuals and for society as a whole. This gives us the definition: *the city is the actions of a densified multitude of different people in a particularly structured unit*. That says something about the conditions under which people act in the city, but nothing about how they act. To achieve that, we must add a fifth feature.

Acting within the city

Varying definitions of "the city" have been inscribed in different languages. They reflect regional experiences and cultural achievements.

Table 11. Specific semantic content

LANGUAGE	SPECIFIC SEMANTIC CONTENT: THE CITY IS…
Egyptian	… dense infrastructure
Greek	… (citizen) politics
Latin	… (power) politics
Spanish	… structured density
French	… an own lifestyle
English	… a form of particular relevance and function
German	… rights
Russian	… a centre
Arabic	… civilization
Hindi	… prosperity
Chinese	… the economy
Japanese	… a hub and a particular lifestyle

We cannot see the commonalities until we go back to where we started: To which question is the city the answer? Now we can see that all of the above concepts describe a particular way of acting. We thus not only know something about the city as a framework for urban action, but also about the urban acts themselves.

This leads us to the theory of action. The approach adopted by the sociologist *Hans Joas*, who believes that action is *creative*, is illuminating in this respect.[58] Without going into any more detail, this is, of course, a very broad interpretation. If all action is creative, the concept becomes arbitrary. For that reason, we need to differentiate creative acts from everyday acts. Everyday acts must be *timely* and *efficient*, for example routine grocery shopping, going to work etc. More is needed for acts to be creative. A creative action is performed when everyday acts are insufficient. Action is creative when it finds *new, innovative,* and surprising solutions and establishes a *pioneering method*.

---

58 Joas, Hans (2005, original 1992), The Creativity of Action, trans. Jeremy Gaines and Paul Keast. Cambridge.

Table 12. Action[59]

Criterion	Meaning
CREATIVE ACTION	
New, innovative	"New" means recently found or discovered, or also a combination of known responses. "Innovative" can be understood as progressive, e.g. the managed improvement of a product, a social system etc. That explains the difference to new, because not all that is new is also innovative.
Surprising	An unexpected response, when standard responses are insufficient. Also: the inspiring moment of the unexpected or astounding.
Pioneering	A surprising and innovative act changes the way people acted before and establishes a new method as the standard.
EVERYDAY ACTION	
Timely	… an own lifestyle
Efficient	… a form of special relevance and function

If we see the experiences inscribed within the various languages as the result of creative action, we open up a new perspective. Creativity plays an important role. That does not, however, mean that action that takes place within a city is of itself creative, or that it is more creative than actions performed in rural areas. The difference is that creative action under the conditions of densification lead to results that are characteristic only of the city. In other words, *the city is a structured, diverse, enclosed unit of creative densification.* To analyse the value of this result, we must leave the field of theory. Nothing is more practical than a good theory for understanding reality. Time for a practical stress test.

---

[59] As a rule, "creativity" is used positively, but any number of destructive actions can rightly call themselves creative. It follows that actions linked to or performed within the city are as ambivalent as human actions everywhere.

IV. PRACTICE

A. Zooming in

Anyone who follows the debate about cities is consistently confronted with two lines of discussion. There are certain issues that are constantly discussed by everyone, everywhere: work, health, housing, real estate and rent prices, transportation, analogue and digital infrastructure, culture, sports etc. They are constantly being covered by all media channels, and what people say about them makes for the background noise to how people feel about the city, usually one's own city.

But the gold standard of these debates are the disputes around the terms used to describe the city, the concepts of the city, and the different city types. These debates are not common, but when they do come up, they are often heated. To name just one example, almost every mayor today is willing to invest huge sums to ensure their city is considered a *smart city*. City types form a level which connects the city as a whole with individual issues. Typologizing reduces complexity and provides orientation by creating order. Clarity and the ability to make judgements are particularly important in this area. Yet there are, of course, often other interests at play that are not immediately apparent, but that are nevertheless important

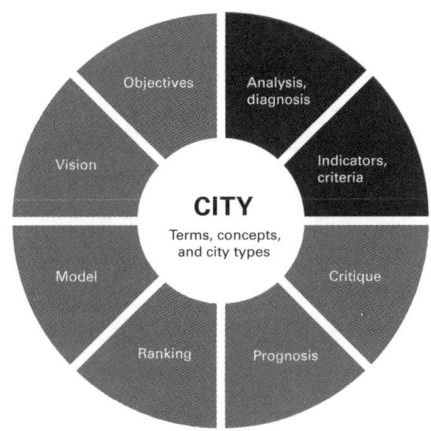

Figure 6. Functions of city types.

on account of their huge impact. If they are effective, they can mobilize an urban society to act in a certain way over a long period of time. The *car-friendly city* is perhaps the most influential 20th-century example.

Things can get confusing, because new terms, concepts, and city types are constantly being developed by people working in research, business, and politics. To gain clarity, we need to delve more deeply into the different concepts. This is a three-step process:

1) First we have to clarify the function of each city type. That allows us to clarify which areas a particular type covers and – at least as important – which areas it does *not* cover.

   That way, we can identify the aims and interests linked to each city type.

   A recent handbook on the topic provides a good overview of the functions of the city.[60] In their introduction, the authors pinpoint eight fields (see *Figure 6*), which can be used as a grid that places the concept of the city developed in the theory section of this book in context. Two areas are key here, that is *indicators* and *criteria* for *analysis* and *diagnosis* purposes. This point of view seeks to record reality – while *objectives*, *models*, *visions* as well as *rankings*, *prognoses*, or *critique* are of only marginal interest. We will apply this process in the following to select city types.

2) In the theory section, we defined "city" as *creative, densified diversity within a structured unit*. In a second step we will look at whether and how city types incorporate these features. We will also look at how they interact. As a result, we can see whether, by emphasizing one feature, we are ignoring another, and then identify the consequences of doing that.

3) City types provide answers to questions. These questions are, in turn, not always clearly formulated. In a third and final step, we will attempt to do just that.

Table 13. Functions, form, and content

FUNCTIONS	
Analysis and diagnosis | Indicators and criteria	
FEATURES	
FORM Conditions for acting within the city	CONTENT Acting within the city

– Structure
– Diversity
– Unity
– Densification
	– Creativity
	  • Creative action: new and innovative; surprising; methodologically groundbreaking
	  • Everyday actions: timely and efficient

After looking at city types, we will turn our attention to some issues that are central to cities. Concentrating on issues can help us to focus, but it can also narrow our gaze. If you focus on the environment, you might be ignoring the economy, and vice versa. If you focus on the digital transformation, you might be up to date technologically, but will be ignoring that segment of the population that cannot afford, or use, or rejects this cultural technology. While that might not interest many people, they too will pay the price down the line. Those, in turn,

---

60 Rink, Dieter; Haase, Annegret (eds.) (2008), Handbuch Stadtkonzepte. Analysen, Diagnosen, Kritiken und Visionen. Opladen, Toronto, p. 12.

who would rather abolish or even ban certain technologies are missing a trick. And those – as a third and final example – who are interested only in security may restrict people's liberties to such an extent that there is nothing left worth protecting. In contrast, those who do not take security seriously should not be surprised if one day they become the victim.

In short, we will be looking at issues that are important to cities, but not only to cities. Our aim is to recognize their logic and to investigate the question of what these issues do to cities and, vice versa, what influence the city has on these issues. Here, too, the features we identified in the theory section will act as our guide. Let us begin with the intermediate level.

B. Terms, concepts, and city types

Terms, concepts, and city types are trading high. Sometimes they seem like stock market commodities whose value rises and falls with economic cycles. There are so many that it is almost impossible to get an overview, much less to evaluate them all. The sample investigated here was based on the following reflection:

One of the most important developments is urban growth, both in terms of the number of cities and their size. In 100 CE there was only one city with a population of one million, that is *Rome*. In 1000 CE, there was still only one city of that size, namely *Angkor Wat* in *Cambodia*. With industrialization, the number of cities over one million rose from four to 12 over the course of the 19th century. In 2020, the number of cities with over one million inhabitants was exactly 500.[61] That list is headed by *megacities*. That is the first city type we will look at. Closely related but not identical to the megacity is a new city type – the *global city*. Global cities have incomparable influence. Smaller cities, too, are of course unable to avoid being sucked into the competition-oriented economization of all areas of life across the whole of the world. The global city builds on the concept of the *neoliberal city*.

While global cities steer the global economy, there is no political body that is equal to this city type. But one of the oldest *city types* is still relatively powerful, that is the *capital city*.

The *arrival city* is the answer to another important global issue in that it is the first port of call for immigrants along global migration routes. If the prognoses are to be believed, these cities will gain in importance in the coming years.

And while we are thinking about the future, one of the urban models that is currently drawing the most attention is the *smart city*. In this concept, the economy and environmental protection are brought together through technological innovations.

Where there are winners, there are also losers. Places that are threatened by disaster, like the global pandemic that broke out in 2019, or places that are shrinking. Shrinking is commonly considered to be a crisis. When the opportu-

---

61 en.wikipedia.org/wiki/List_of_largest_cities (accessed: 23 Apr. 2022).

nities inherent to every crisis go unused, it becomes a disaster. Finally, we will turn to the *virus city*, the *shrinking city*, and the *lost city*.

The objective of this brief selection of city types is, on the one hand, to examine the latest trends as important current phenomena and, on the other hand, to provide examples of the application of a method of investigating the substance of individual types so that we can determine not only what they are made of, but also how robust they are.

(i) *A note on methodology*

I'd first like to say something about my method. The previous section shifted attention to the function of different terms for, concepts of, and types of cities. To determine the function that is associated with each concept, the functions were evaluated according to a point system. The points were distributed on the basis of my own and others' analyses as follows:

- ••• The term, concept, or city type is associated one-to-one with a certain function.
- •• The function is pronounced.
- • The function is discernible.
- – The function is not discernible.

---

1. Megacity

The megacity is currently the largest urban unit. For most of the history of humankind people have lived in the countryside. It has only been 7,000 years since the first human beings, initially very few, lived in cities. In the mid-20th century, around one third of the global population was living in urban areas. This percentage exploded in the second half of the century, reaching a historical tipping point in less than two generations. In 2007, global rural and urban populations were, for a brief moment in history, perfectly balanced. But it was, for the moment, a waystation and urbanization continues, with the megacity at the spearhead of this development.

Researchers are not agreed on exactly when a city becomes a megacity. Cities with populations of more than five million are usually considered to be *emerging megacities*, and become full-fledged megacities at the latest when the number of inhabitants surpasses 10 million. Currently, there are over 29 urban areas with a population of over 10 million and 73 with more than five million inhabitants.[62]

---

62 Kabisch, Sigrun; Kraas, Frauke (2018), Megastadt, in: Rink, Dieter; Haase, Annegret (eds.) (2018), p. 216.

Table 14. Development of the global population and urban population

	YEAR	POPULATION		
		WORLD (IN BILLIONS)	CITIES (IN BILLIONS)	SHARE OF CITIES
BCE	75000	1,000–10,000 survive the Toba disaster		
	10000	0.004		
CE	0	0.170–0.400		
	500	0.190		
	1000	0.310		
	1500	0.5000		
	1815	1.000		
	1950	2.540	0.750	29.6%
	1960	3.030	1.020	33.7%
	1970	3.700	1.350	36.5%
	2000	6.140	2.860	46.6%
	2007	6.670	3.340	50.0%
	2015	7.380	3.960	54.0%

Step 1: What kind of city is the megacity?

Looking at functions enables us to make an initial assessment. In sharp contrast to the *smart city*, for example, the megacity is neither a *model* nor the result of any *objectives* set – and it is certainly not the embodiment of any *vision*. Rather, it is a harsh and very confusing reality. The concept of the megacity can, therefore, be the subject of *analyses* and *diagnoses*, to some extent of *prognoses,* and, depending on the question, of *critique*.

Table 15. Functions of the megacity

Analysis, diagnosis	Indicators, criteria	Critique	Prognosis	Ranking	Model	Vision	Objectives
•••	–	•	••	–	–	–	–

Step 2: What are the features of the megacity?

Aside from population size, there is disagreement as to the characteristics of this city type. *Table 16* lists some of the features that are most frequently mentioned.[63] The picture gets clearer when these features are compared to those that every city possesses. The main feature after population is, of course, *density*. *Diversity* and *creative action* are also frequently mentioned.

Table 16. Features of the megacity

1)	Population > 5 or 10 million
2)	High population density
3)	Fast pace of change
4)	Demographic shift towards a growing and younger population
5)	Large social disparities and highly differentiated socio-spatial living conditions
6)	Significant infrastructural deficits
7)	Limited ability to steer development

Strangely, diversity is usually only implicit in definitions provided in the literature, usually on account of an emphasis being placed on the intense momentum of change or the decreasing median age of the population. Most descriptions concentrate on the conditions within which actions take place. The literature usually only refers to the actions themselves by citing examples. This is true for both everyday acts and for creative solutions. However, these examples are not brought together to increase our analytical understanding. Yet creative acts cannot be ignored, especially in megacities. Examined more closely, they are often remarkable, even if they do not always correspond to the usual definition of creative action.

There is, however, one type of action that is always cited in reference to megacities, namely *informal acts*, that is that part of the urban economy that is not included in official statistics and is therefore also not taxed. It includes both criminal activity as well as acts by those people who are excluded from the legal economy and who have hardly any other options for surviving in a megacity. Put in academic language: "In the form of self-help and self-organization, it represents an alternative to the limited absorption capacity of the formal sector."[64]

Finally, two developmental paths are notable that are both writ large in the megacity. Both are the result of the actions of very different population groups.

---

63 Bronger, Dirk (2004), Metropolen, Megastädte, Global Cities. Die Metropolisierung der Erde. Darmstadt, p. 31–35. Using the term "*Metropole*" (metropolis), Bronger provides a powerful example of the "Babylonian confusion in German urban research" (p. 30).
64 Kabisch, Sigrun; Kraas, Frauke (2018), p. 226. The following quotation: p. 230.

Some areas of the megacity become an *arrival city*, which we will look at more closely later on. At the same time, these cities are also *global cities*, which we will also examine in more detail, whose main function is as a "command centre" of the global economy.

It is almost impossible to summarize what is characteristic of the *infrastructure* of a megacity. The differences between cities that have sufficient resources, such as *New York City* and *Tokyo*, and cities in India, Asia, Africa, and South America, are simply too great. It is very difficult to draw any generalized conclusions about this city type.

Table 17. Prevalence of urban features in the megacity

Conditions for action				Action
Densification	Diversity	Infrastructure	Unity	Creativity
•••	••	•	–	••

In sum, it is difficult to still regard megacities as a *unit*. Administrative, economic, and perhaps cultural factors back up this point of view, but the concept of the city reaches its limits here. "Megacity" is thus above all a quantitative description. It is size that makes a city of millions a megacity – "a highly complex and highly dynamic living environment for many people", as Sigrun Kabisch and Frauke Kraas put it in their well-founded analysis, "that promises opportunities for a better life, but is also rife with risks".

Step 3: To which question is the megacity the answer?

Up until the 1980s, the future of cities, especially large cities, appeared precarious. The coldness of "steel and glass" (*John Lennon*) became a metaphor for a lifestyle with no future. During this phase, industrial flight was rampant, people lost their jobs, municipalities lost out on revenue and their fiscal options, and no small number went bankrupt.

For a long time, nobody saw the opportunities that were inherent in this shift. Artists were among the first to do so, with Andy Warhol leading the way. In 1962, he founded his legendary *Factory* in *New York City*, an abandoned warehouse that he used as an atelier, film studio, party location, and apartment – in short, an experimental playground for the creative community. For almost two decades it was the blueprint for a new kind of urban culture, a lifestyle that was appropriated and economized by the creative economy. Concurrently, the economy

A comprehensive thematic overview is available in:
Assmann, Ulrike; Born, Lukas; Kochendörfer, Bernd; Pahl-Weber, Elke; Zehner, Carsten (eds.) (2014), Future Megacities. Berlin. Vol. 1: Energy and Sun; Vol. 2: Mobility and Transportation; Vol. 3: Capacity Development; Vol. 4: Local Action and Participation: Space, Planning, and Design.

Kleer, Jerzy; Nawrot, Katarzyna Anna (eds.) (2018), The Rise of Megacities. Challenges, Opportunities and Unique Characteristics. London. *The most recent, best, and most comprehensive anthology.*

shifted from production to services. This development rapidly gathered pace in the 1990s with the opening of financial markets, *globalization*, and *the digital transformation*. Unexpectedly and contrary to the original prognoses, cities are making a comeback. The cultural avant-garde has made cities attractive for new forms of living and working. These forms are meant to draw in the right kind of people, to create new jobs and a new kind of lifestyle.

But it would be a simplification to see in this development merely the fall and rise of the city. The process is, in truth, more complicated. While highly-skilled jobs were created, so were considerably more marginal, low-paid jobs, often even illegal work that generates no tax revenue. That above all holds true for the *global city*. While these jobs symbolize the middle classes' fear of a loss of social status, for immigrants who lived under worse conditions in their home countries they represent, if not their dreams, then at least a promise of a better life, which makes it worth leaving one's old life behind.

This dual process explains the radical growth of cities over recent decades – and their magnetic appeal. In that respect, the megacity is the answer to the promise of a piece of the pie that is the new economy. The fact that this promise cannot be fulfilled for everyone does little to change that, in the same way that cities are no longer truly able to control the consequences of this development.

2. Global city

Not every megacity is necessarily a global city. The latter term was already examined in our exploration of *Saskia Sassen*'s eponymous book (see III.B.7), and hence needs no further clarification. Let us, therefore, look directly at the *global city*'s functions. The term is usually used in the context of *analyses* and *diagnoses* of urban *globalization* and has exact *indicators* and *criteria*. The concept is also useful when it comes to creating *rankings*. It can also be seen as a *model* or as the result of *objectives*, and, to a certain extent, *prognoses* can be made about global cities.

Table 18. Functions of the global city

Analysis, diagnosis	Indicators, criteria	Critique	Prognosis	Ranking	Model	Vision	Objectives
•••	••	–	•	•••	••	•	••

In this city type, some of the features are very pronounced, while others are not discernible at all. *Densification* and *diversity* are only interesting to the extent that they support the main functions. Highly specialized segments of the infrastructure, those needed for global financial markets, for example, are, by contrast, more pronounced than in any other city type. That goes along with *creative* action for which specific skills are needed. *Unity*, by contrast, plays no role at all. In fact, this feature acts as an obstacle to the most important functions of the global city.

Bundling global control functions in a small space, for example key financial institutions such as central banks and transnational companies, attracts the relevant services that settle nearby. These include legal and financial services, business consultants, ad agencies, accounting services, and high-end cultural and recreational facilities. They are supplemented by numerous low-end services such as couriers, and cleaning and security services.

While in the 1990s the main focus was on steering global financial markets, management functions have now expanded beyond this sector to include globalized industrial production. Management functions have even set their sights on the area of cultural production.

These global steering mechanisms have another consequence. This city type no longer refers solely to the region or nation-state in which the city is located, but must be analysed "within the framework of *globalization* … as part of a global system of cities."[65] Analyses usually concentrate on factors that can be easily determined, for example the *number of company headquarters* in a city. Based on these factors it is possible to create rankings, an easily understood measuring tool that is used around the world. The simplicity of rankings most likely explains their popularity and makes it easy to use them to set new objectives.

Table 19. Prevalence of urban features in the global city

	Conditions for action			Action
Densification	Diversity	Infrastructure	Unity	Creativity
•	•	•••	–	•••

Inner rifts are a further consequence of being a "global city". Of course, social differences are endemic to all cities for very different reasons. But a global city needs these differences in order to function. When it comes to the population and, using the jargon of the social sciences, this means that "a differentiation is made between the 'transnational' segment of the urban population – that is those inhabitants that maintain multiple continuing social relationships across national borders – and those urban inhabitants who are *not* involved in transnational social relationships."[66] In other words, two highly specialized experts in the same sector living in Shanghai and New York are often closer to one another because of both their work and their lifestyle than they are to their local carpenter – should the latter have been able to keep her business going. There have been many detailed descriptions of this development, encapsulated, for example, in the concept of the *dual city*, or *divided city*.

---

65   Krätke, Stefan (2018), in: Rink, Dieter; Haase, Annegret (eds.) (2018), p. 129.
66   Krätke, Stefan (2018), p. 133. Emphasis in the original.

> *The global city as a strategy*
>
> The concept of the global city is now linked to the myriad interests of the economic, political, cultural, and academic sectors. The global city as a strategy is, as one of the most recent and comprehensive synopses claims, "usually aimed at achieving a prestigious ranking as a 'global city' to better its position in the global competition between cities. The concept of the global city hence becomes remodelled into a new variant of growth ideology and as such acts as political legitimation for urban development projects."[67]

The *global city* thus describes the phenomenon of an economy that acts transnationally and is, increasingly, digitally networked and oriented to efficiency and profits. It offers transnational companies a platform. While *New York City*, *London*, and *Tokyo* were the first to be classed as global cities, there is now a broad spectrum with numerous sub-types.

In the course of this development, many cities that just a generation ago held a prominent position within their respective national systems have now lost in significance. This is initially true of industrial centres such as the *Ruhr region* in Germany, port cities such as *Marseille*, or cities with large populations such as *Lagos*. Simultaneously, cities like *Singapore*, *Hong Kong*, *Seoul*, and *Manila* have become up-and-coming subcentres by specializing in the direct management of transnational production networks. Global cities – like some transnational companies – have become global players in the field of *international relations* and much more influential than most states.

While megacities are characterized by their size and global cities by their economic role, the main feature of the next city type is its political function.

> Ljungkvist, Kristin (2016), The Global City 2.0. From strategic site to global actor. London. *Solid theoretical analysis using the empirical example of New York City.*
>
> Scott, Alen J. (2001), Global City-Regions. Trends, Theory, Policy. Oxford. *High-quality anthology of well-respected authors.*

3. Capital city

There are a limited number of capital cities and yet their number is difficult to pin down. There are 195 United Nations member states, plus *Palestine* and *Vatican City* (which enjoy special status). All of these countries have at least one capital. There are a further 10 countries that are not yet UN members because other countries do not recognize them. In some countries, the capital is not the seat of government. One example is the *Netherlands*: while *Amsterdam* is the capital, the *king* and the *government* are based in *Den Haag*. There are even countries that have no formal capital, for example *Switzerland*: *Bern* is the "*federal city*", but is not, by law, a capital city. *Liechtenstein* is another example. It does not

---

67 Krätke, Stefan (2018), p. 143. On the dual and divided city, see Rast, Joel (2019), The Origins of the Dual City: Housing, Race & Redevelopment in Twentieth-Century Chicago. Chicago. Singh, Binti; Sethi, Mahendra (2018), The Divided City: Ideological and Policy Contestations in Contemporary Urban India. Singapore.

have *any* cities at all. *Vaduz* fulfils the function of a capital, but it was never granted city rights.

These facts are all easily available and can be sorted into any number of informative clusters in tables.[68] As an example, *Table 20* lists the five largest and the five smallest capital cities.

Table 20. Top five capital cities

	THE FIVE BIGGEST…			THE FIVE SMALLEST…	
CITY	COUNTRY	POP.	CITY	COUNTRY	POP.
Beijing	China	21,730,000	San Marino	San Marino	4,036
Tokyo	Japan	13,159,400	Castries	St. Lucia	3,662
Kinshasa	DR Congo	11,575,000	Vatican City	Vatican City	750
Moscow	Russia	11,514,300	Yaren	Nauru	750
Seoul	Korea	9,794,300	Palau	Ngerulmud	277

It appears that no one has yet undertaken the laborious task of counting all the capitals of all the constituent states, for example federal states, across the world. The number most likely is somewhere in the thousands. With a global total of several tens of thousands of cities that have a population of more than 100,000, the only thing we can say for sure today is that capital cities only make up a small percentage of all cities. This makes them a rare and exclusive city type.

Step 1: What kind of city is the capital city?

A capital city is the place from which a *country*, a *federated state*, or *region* is governed. In most cases, it is the seat of the most important constitutional and governmental bodies as well as other administrative bodies. They are meant not only to manage but also to represent their constituencies, occasionally they even have a vision. These are usually created on the federal and not the municipal level, but the former expresses its self-image through the latter in the form of facilities and buildings.

When it comes to the areas that pertain to this city type, we can exclude *analysis* and *diagnosis* as well as *ranking*. There are individual cases in which capitals compete with one another in terms of their representative pomp and splendour, but the differences between them are so great that it does not make much sense to compare them.

On account of their function, *indicators* and *criteria* do play a role in regard to capital cities. So that the head of state, the government and its adminis-

---

[68] en.wikipedia.org/wiki/Capital_city#Capitals_that_are_not_the_seat_of_government (accessed: 23 Apr. 2022).

trations, and the highest court can all fulfil their duties, skilled specialist staff, buildings, and analogue and digital *infrastructure* are all necessary. The people who work in government also need housing, as well as utilities and recreational facilities.

Table 21. Functions of the capital city

Analysis, diagnosis	Indicators, criteria	Critique	Prognosis	Ranking	Model	Vision	Objectives
–	••	•	•	–	••	•	••

Finally, the capital city's function as a *model* is also important. This is often linked to certain *objectives*, even though they can often only be loosely covered by the term "representative". It is rare for a capital city to embody contemporary *visions*. Trust in societal identity seems to be decreasing along with the design of capital cities as a promise for the future. Both are the result of either obsolete ideas or drastically lowered expectations. Further, in the age of *globalization*, states hardly ever seem to have a self-image to which they need to give form through visionary architectural designs in capital cities or even to make them possible in light of the dynamic developments in all areas.

One of the rare examples is the transformation of *Berlin* into the capital city of reunified Germany. Old buildings from previous governments were reactivated, such as the Reichstag Building as the seat of Parliament, supplemented by modern buildings such as the Federal Chancellery. But the country does not seem so sure about what to do with the city centre, and has opted for a course of musealization, reconstructing the former Berlin Palace on its old ground plan but in a modern form. That is hardly visionary. And so creativity is currently focusing on other things. Here are three examples:

- In *Mecca*, an enormous complex, a place of pilgrimage, is being built around the *Kaaba*, the religious centre of Islam.
- A futuristic and visionary complex for business and recreation is being built in *Dubai*. With a 40-kilometre radius, it includes the tallest building in the world, the Burj Khalifa (828 metres), and 47 other buildings with a height of more than 250 metres. At the time of writing, one building is in construction that is planned to be more 1,000 metres tall.
- The Basilica Notre Dame de la Paix was built in *Yamoussoukro*, the capital of *Ivory Coast* between 1985 and 1988. The church borrows heavily from St. Peter's Basilica in the Vatican City.

In each of these cases, the city becomes an *object* of and a *platform* for sacral or economic ideas.

In future, two more issues will gain in importance: epidemics and pandemics as well as climate change. The former paralyzed cities around the globe in

2020 in an unprecedented manner and forced capital cities to work in new ways. This danger can return at any time.

Table 22. Planned capital cities[69]

	KARLSRUHE	GERMANIA	BRASILIA
Time	1715	1937–43	1891 | 1922 | 1956–60
Country	Germany	Germany	Brazil
Claim	"Built like a star … clear and full of light like a rule … as if an orderly mind is speaking to us." Heinrich von Kleist	"Berlin will be comparable as a world capital only to Egypt, Babylon, or Rome." *Adolf Hitler*	"What does draw me is the free and sensual curve … that I find in the mountains of my country, in the sinuousness of her rivers, in the clouds of the sky." *Oscar Niemeyer*
Figs. 7–9			
Implementation	From the palace 32 streets fan out in a circle like "the rays of the sun." *Friedrich Weinbrenner's* classical design is influential, inspired by *antiquity* and its Prussian, above all Berlin, interpretation.	In parts incorporates buildings planned during the Weimar Republic. Most well-known structures include the *Olympic Stadium, Tempelhof Airport* and the *Reich Ministry of Aviation* (now housing the Federal Ministry of Finance).	Modern design 1956–1960. Oscar Niemeyer created the emblematic public buildings. The centre of Brasilia was originally seen as a masterpiece of modernity, but the city lacks the vibrancy of a capital city.
Today	Pop. 300,000, second largest city in the federal state of Baden-Württemberg. The city's ground plan and Weinbrenner's design remain.	Plans and models have survived, along with some buildings and the East–West axis.	UNESCO World Heritage site since 1987. Now showing signs of decay.
Critique | Impact	*Thomas Jefferson* visited the city in 1788. His enthusiasm led to elements of Karlsruhe's ground plan being incorporated into plans for Washington D.C.	"My theory is that monumental architecture is prison architecture. The city becomes a prison that you can always march out of and that you return to." *Klaus Heinrich*	"Widely considered a failed experiment." *Oscar Niemeyer*

---

69 Kleist cited in Schenk, Günter (2017), CityTrip Karlsruhe. Bielefeld, p. 100. Hitler cited in Berliner Unterwelten e.V., The Myth of Germania, 2005 exhibition, trans. Allison Brown. Oscar Niemeyer cited in Emanuel, Muriel (ed.) (2016), Contemporary Architects. UK, p. 589. Heinrich cited in Heinrich, Klaus (2015), p. 186.

> Schultz, Uwe (ed.) (1993), Die Hauptstädte der Deutschen. Von der Kaiserpfalz in Aachen zum Regierungssitz in Berlin. Munich. *Comprehensive overview by renowned authors.*
>
> Menasse, Robert (2020), The Capital, trans. Jamie Bulloch. London. *An informative novel about the European Union (EU) capital Brussels.*

And many capital cities are threatened by climate change, for example *Jakarta* in *Indonesia*. In 2019, the government announced it will be leaving the capital, which has been sinking by around 25 centimetres each year. The new capital will be in East Kalimantan on the island of *Borneo*. The first sentence of the announcement of this step could have been formulated in almost the same way by 18th- or 19th-century rulers: "A capital city is not only a symbol of national identity, it also represents a nation's progress. This step is a step towards economic equality and justice."[70]

Step 2: What are the features of the capital city?

Capital cities are places with a function. First, they have to manage a large area: a country or a federal state. Second, they have to embody the self-image of the territory they represent. The third function stems from the first and is expressed in the second. That means that the management of a territory occurs, on the one hand, through standard administrative procedures, as well as through special programmes, measures, and projects. These pilot projects are often implemented in the capital city. It is by means of these processes that the capital becomes a *platform* for politics.

Managing territory, symbolizing a national identity, and serving as a platform are the capital's three most important political functions. In addition, capital cities are often regional or national economic, scientific, and cultural centres. While that is not an original feature, it is almost always true of European capitals, most of which can be traced back to former royal residences. In many countries, the division of labour between several cities evolved over time or was consciously promoted.

Clear priorities can be seen if one examines those features that are characteristic of a capital city. Most important is the *infrastructure* created for this city type and the *actions* within it.

Densification and *diversity* are important for capital cities only in relation to action. The diversity of the tasks and the division of labour across the different areas in capitals usually brings about conflicts and creative solutions. Assessing the results would, however, require us to compare the systems of government the capitals serve. To my knowledge, no one has yet undertaken a systematic analysis of this topic on a global level, though such a comparison would certainly be fascinating, if perhaps linked to numerous value judgements.

---

70   tagesschau.de/ausland/indonesien-341.html (accessed: 23 Apr. 2022).

Table 23. Prevalence of urban features in the capital city

	Conditions for action			Action	
Densification	Diversity	Infrastructure	Unity	Creativity
•	•	•••	••	•••

Let us turn again to the feature *unity*. It is of great significance for capital cities – across all systems of government. The most common global systems operate with four powers (head of state, government, parliament, and judiciary). Even authoritarian states often have a semblance of a balance of powers. While the interactions between these elements vary greatly, ideally, at least in theory, they combine to form a *unit*.

Step 3: To which question is the capital city the answer?

The capital city can be understood as the answer to the need to manage larger territories. It is the default solution for this task. Seen in this way, capital cities are a type of infrastructure that promotes creative action.

Put more abstractly, the capital city is the answer to the invention of space and the need or the will to rule it. Or, put less bluntly, to manage it. Without going into the long and controversial debates on the rise of civilizations, it can safely be asserted that this development went hand in hand with spatial and social differentiation. That, in turn, needs to be managed, which is what a capital city does, regardless of the aims or motives of the management, as *Michael Mann* has investigated at length in his multi-volume *The Sources of Social Power*.[71]

A way of better evaluating the role of capital cities is to ask how they are used by different countries. As a rule, they act as a *platform* for the respective countries and their governments to express their identity. During conflicts between countries or governmental systems, cities sometimes become their *object*. That does not happen very often, but when it does, it always has far-reaching consequences. Examples that underline this assertion are *Königsberg* after *World War I*, *Berlin* during the *Cold War*, and *Jerusalem* to this day. It is, however, the exception for capital cities to themselves become actors, or *subjects*.

Capital cities are cities that have functions that go far beyond those of a "normal" city. There is another city type with additional functions, a type that is usually seen as an undesirable place. I am referring to *slums* and *ghettos* and comparable areas. Usually, people looking at this city type are examining it from a middle-class perspective. How much this perspective overlooks becomes clear when we turn our gaze to one of the most important city types of our times, that is the arrival city.

---

71   Mann, Michel (1994, original 1986), The Sources of Social Power. Vol. 1. A History of Power from the Beginning to AD 1760. Cambridge.

4. Arrival city

The Canadian–British journalist *Doug Saunders* has studied one of the most dynamic developments of the present: urban migration. He predicts that "we will end this century as a wholly urban species",[72] and asks both how this migration functions and what are its effects.

For Saunders, arrival cities include "the northern reaches of Mumbai, the dusty edges of Tehran, the hillside folds of *São Paulo* and *Mexico City*, the smouldering apartment-block fringes of *Paris* and *Amsterdam* and *Los Angeles*." These are the areas that are usually labelled *poverty-stricken* neighbourhoods or *slums*, and denote places in which migrants are concentrated. Saunders is interested in the people who have chosen these cities as their destination, asking about their motivations, dreams, and how they organize their daily lives. When looking at the cities themselves, the author asks how immigration has changed them and what they have gained.

Step 1: What kind of city is the arrival city?

Drawing on 28 examples, Saunders, a journalist by trade, provides in-depth reports on the neighbourhoods that are used by migrants as a stepping stone to a better life in a more attractive neighbourhood. He provides neither *indicators* nor *criteria*, nor *rankings*, these can at best be extrapolated from his research. What he does offer is an abundance of *critical reflection* and familiarity with the actions of various cities that face these challenges. This allows him to make *prognoses*. These can even be used to derive the beginnings of *model* schemes, as well as the cities' *objectives*. Above all, though, Saunders's concept is an instrument of *analysis* and *diagnosis*.

Table 24. Functions of the arrival city

Analysis, diagnosis	Indicators, criteria	Critique	Prognosis	Ranking	Model	Vision	Objectives
•••	–	••	•	–	••	–	–

Step 2: What are the features of the arrival city?

The most important feature of arrival cities is their *diversity* as a result of migration. For Saunders, this is neither negative nor positive; he believes each case should be assessed individually. In the main, migration is a phenomenon that is caused by poverty. The local population and the immigrant population encountering each other is never without its conflicts. Through detailed descriptions of such conflicts, the author illustrates how differently arrival cities can develop. While they are often first of all "spaces of optimism", as Doug Saunders puts

---

72 Saunders, Doug (2011), Arrival City. New York, p. 1–2. The following quotations: ibid., p. 523–527.

it, they can also become areas of system-busting squalor.

This perspective tends to obscure the positive impacts of migration. Saunders describes a great number of such slums, such as *Dharavi* in *Mumbai*, *Orangi Town* in *Karachi*, *Ashaiman* in *Ghana*, and *Villa el Salvador* in *Peru*, and he comes to the conclusion that while these places began as improvised enclaves, today they are successful economic regions with numerous factories, and they make a substantial contribution to the national economy.

Infrastructure has a huge influence on how diversity is organized. Interestingly, Saunders does not agree with *Robert Ezra Park* that social relations are "inevitably correlated with spatial relations". Instead, "it is equally possible to become fully integrated, economically and culturally, *within* the confines of the original arrival city. Indeed, a sizable new body of scholarship shows that ethnic 'clustering' can be the most effective pathway to social and economic integration." This theory runs counter to most widely-held views, but it is well-documented and convincing.

Densification does not play the most important role in this process. The focus is on how diversity is organized and on the corresponding actions used to find *creative* solutions. These solutions can originate from the migrants themselves, from the local population, from ideas put forward by committed city planners, suggestions put forward by municipal administrations or other groups. In turn, they have the chance to succeed if they are able to communicate interests clearly and fairly and when these open up attractive opportunities. These positive developments have a positive impact on the city as a whole. The most interesting result of Saunders's observations is that "the functioning arrival city slowly colonizes the established city (just as the failed arrival city is likely, after festering and simmering, to invade it violently). This makes the arrival city "a significant locus of struggle for (urban) citizenship and transformation in urban configuration".

> **ⓘ** *Planet of Slums*
>
> The most popular works on the subject include books by the American sociologist and historian Mike Davis. In *Planet of Slums* (2006) he paints a dark, hopeless picture and creates a nuanced typology of slums using an anti-capitalist approach.
>
> While Davis delivers a plethora of sound facts, the results remain one-dimensional. For him, slum dwellers are victims of an economic system whose promises are only delivered to the few. The only option left for slum inhabitants is rebellion.
>
> And it is here that his analysis differs from Saunders's more nuanced approach. Saunders shows that there are many possibilities for improving living conditions besides rebellion.

Table 25. Prevalence of urban features in the arrival city

	Conditions for action			Action
Densification	Diversity	Infrastructure	Unity	Creativity
••	•••	•	••	••

Step 3: To which question is the arrival city the answer?

The arrival city changes both immigrants *and* long-established residents. The direction this change takes depends on the opportunities that people identify or create. "The crucial paradox of the arrival city is that its occupants all want to stop living in an arrival city – either by making money and moving their families and village networks out or by turning the neighbourhood itself into something better."

The strength of Saunders's study is his focus on something that others have overlooked. It ends with a surprising conclusion: While at first it seemed to be a study of only parts of a city, with each example it becomes clearer that, in reality, the city as a whole is involved. "For the ultimate lesson of the arrival city is that it does not simply add itself on to the edges of the city; it *becomes* the city. Whether it does so creatively or destructively is a matter of engagement."

The arrival city is the urban answer to global migrations. Saunders opens our eyes to the fact that these create not only burdens, but also opportunities This study, which is based on a wealth of experience, is currently one of the most intelligent analyses of this city type, even though the author does not develop his own theory.

If the arrival city starts with a huge problem, for which a surprising solution is developed, the next city type promises much more. Its name alone suggests a solution that is sure to make everyone happy. Whether the *smart city* meets these expectations is the subject of the next section.

📖 Saunders, Doug (2011), Arrival City. New York. *Most comprehensive investigation into arrival cities around the world.*

Davis, Mike (2006), Planet of Slums. London. *Influential analysis of the development of slums from a leftist perspective.*

Dickens, Charles (2003, original 1837–1839), Oliver Twist. London. *An account of slums at the beginning of the industrial revolution. Despite what is, from today's perspective, justified literary criticism, the book remains a gripping read.*

5. Smart city

One of the current best linguistic algorithms cites several dozen meanings and synonyms for the word "smart".[73] The literature concentrates on five or six meanings, whereby *intelligent*, *clever*, *astute*, and *savvy* are seldom missing. This alone makes it clear that "the semantic content of the smart city is broad and therefore also and at the same time vague", as *Jens Libbe*, one of the experts in the field, put it.[74]

---

73 Deepl.com/translator#en/de/smart%OA (accessed: 23 Apr. 2022).
74 Libbe, Jens (2018), p. 431.

> ⓘ *Some meanings of and synonyms for "smart"*
>
> bright, intelligent, astute, clever, sharp, wise, brainy, brilliant, precocious, savvy, canny, crafty, ingenious, sage, acute, genius, keen, knowing, knowledgeable, perceptive, percipient, resourceful, shrewd, streetwise, alert, discerning, educated, erudite, exceptional, genial, learned, scholarly, well-educated, well-read, whiz, witty, whip-smart, quick, perspicacious, insightful, sagacious, cunning, artful, penetrating, gifted, able, experienced, adroit, judicious.

Step 1: What kind of city is the smart city?

The term "smart city" has diverse, vivid meanings, which is why it can be understood to mean many different things. This is a disadvantage for science, but an advantage for marketing, particularly as regards the usual definitions and their naïve, visionary character. Jens Libbe provides two common examples that get to the heart of the term. Both make it clear why it is hard to say what exactly a smart city is.

The smart city is an unusual concept, since in the end it implies no more than institutions coming together to do the work they were set up to do in the most efficient, resource-saving manner possible and using the latest technologies. Such assertions are hardly new. To give just one example, it has been said that when designing the city of the future what is important is the "invigoration of the communal spirit and the civic sense, the utilization of dormant or misdirected forces and of scattered knowledge, the harmony between the spirit of the nation, its views and needs, and those of the state agencies."[75]

If that sounds odd to contemporary ears, that is because the quotation dates back to 1807, and is taken from the legendary *Nassau Memorandum* by *Karl Baron von und zum Stein*. His aim was "the revival of a feeling for the fatherland, independence, and national honour." That was the greatest challenge for an era that had to reinvent itself after the Napoleonic Wars.

> ⓘ *Smart city – definition #1*
>
> "We believe a city to be smart when investments in human and social capital and traditional (transport) and modern (IT) communication infrastructure fuel sustainable economic growth and a high quality of life, along with the management of natural resources through participatory governance."

> ⓘ *Smart city – definition #2*
>
> "'Smart city' hence denotes a city that systematically employs information and communication technologies, as well as low-impact technologies, to pave a way towards a post-fossil society, to reduce resource use, to achieve long-term improvements in the life quality of citizens and the competitive advantage of business – in a nutshell, to improve the sustainability of the city. Usually this applies to, at the least, the energy, mobility, urban planning, and governance sectors. An elementary feature of the smart city is that these areas are integrated and networked. Key to this process is the comprehensive integration of social aspects of urban society and public participation."[76]

---

75 Karl Baron von und zum Stein: https://ghdi.ghi-dc.org/docpage.cfm?docpage_id=3790 (accessed: 23 Apr. 2022).
76 Definitions #1 and #2: Libbe, Jens (2018), p. 432.

Back then, the focus was also on the future – the future of the state and the future of the city. The objective of the smart city is no different. It describes the city of tomorrow and offers a *model*, an *objective*, and a *vision*. To measure current efforts in this direction, *rankings* of smart cities are already available.[77] The concept only delivers *analysis* and *critique* when these help to provide the grounds for aims pursued by this concept. But by developing an approach into a future-oriented scheme, it analyses and criticizes the present without providing a ready-made concept. The only thing that is truly novel about the concept of the smart city is the use of innovative technologies as a kind of "master tool", especially digitalization.

Table 26. Functions of the smart city

Analysis, diagnosis	Indicators, criteria	Critique	Prognosis	Ranking	Model	Vision	Objectives
•	–	•	–	••	••	•••	••

Step 2: What are the features of the smart city?

The term "smart city" transfers the contemporary debate around modernization to the city. It is used as an example to simulate what the society of tomorrow should, could, and must look like. One would expect the impetus to come from *philosophy*, the source of so many utopias in the Early Modern period. But that field currently distinguishes itself in the main through dystopias. So many people in the economic, marketing, and political sectors, and parts of academia, have filled in the lacunae in philosophy, offering their own positive visions. Seen in this way, the smart city is a specific kind of social criticism. Spurred on by the idea that the present needs to be actively changed, its critique wrapped up a colourful vision of the future.

The concept became popular due to its ability to co-opt and overarch a number of related concepts. While those concepts concentrate on individual aspects, the idea of the smart city is so broad and so general that it can accommodate them all.

Table 27. The smart city and related concepts

SMART CITY		
Environmental focus	Tools & methods focus	Knowledge focus
– *Sustainable city*	– *Digital city*	– *Intelligent city*
– *Green city*	– *Ubiquitous city*	– *Wired city*
– *Low-carbon city*	[data-protected city]	– *Learning city*
– *Climate-adapted city*	– *Informational city*	– *Creative city*
– *Zero emissions city*		– *Cognitive city*
– *Eco-city*		– *Knowledge city*

---

77 smart-cities.eu/download/smart_cities_final_report.pdf (accessed: 23 Apr. 2022).

In order to assess what the essence of the concept of the smart city is, it is necessary to look at the prevalence of the features of this city type. It is revealing to look at what the smart city does not value. The *unity* of the city plays no role in this concept. It at most appears indirectly in recent debates on opportunities for participation in urban life for all inhabitants, or at least for as many as possible.

> ⓘ *Urban citizens and illiteracy*
>
> UNESCO estimates the number of illiterate people at currently 757 million. In Germany alone, 6.2 million (of a total population of 83 million) are illiterate. The percentage of functional illiterates in the 18- to 64-year-old age group is as high as 12.1%.[78]

When it comes to the *digital transformation*, most proponents of the concept are referring only to a part of the urban popu-lation. By making digitalization a prerequisite for participation in urban life, they are cutting off some urban residents from the ability to be active citizens. This is clearest when we think of those who are unable to read and write or do so only at a rudimentary level. These people are dependent on direct person-to-person contact with municipal administrations. A concept of the city that depends mostly or completely on one tool, in this case digital solutions, excludes these people.

This should not be misunderstood as a critique of modernization, and certainly not as a rejection of the digital transformation, which is most certainly a solution to numerous problems. But it is not a panacea, merely a tool like any other that has its advantages and disadvantages. The smart city's fundamental weakness that becomes apparent here is its tendency to be one-sided. While it claims to be shaping the city of the future, it already excludes a large number of urban inhabitants in mapping its goal. In other words, for the smart city, the unity of the city is not important.

Neither do *diversity* or *densification* play a key role in the concept of the smart city. What is important, though, is *structure*, especially *infrastructure*. It has become clear by now that this refers first and foremost to digital infrastructure. The aim of building networks is clearly formulated. The objective is *efficiency* and – the term is frequently used – *intelligence*. In the broadest sense, the concept includes original and, it must be said, creative solutions. Most authors are reminded of clusters and interdisciplinary cooperation.

Table 28. Prevalence of urban features in the smart city

	Conditions for action			Action
Densification	Diversity	Infrastructure	Unity	Creativity
–	•	••	–	••

---

78 bpb.de/politik/hintergrund-aktuell/211776/weltalphabetisierungstag (accessed: 23 Apr. 2022).

📖 Deakin, Mark; Mora, Luca (2019), Untangling Smart Cities: From utopian dreams to innovation systems for a technology-enabled urban sustainability. Amsterdam. *Currently the best overview.*

Gassmann, Oliver; Böhm, Jonas; Palmié, Maximilian (2018), Smart City. Innovationen für die vernetzte Stadt. Geschäftsmodelle und Management. Munich. *Comprehensive but uncritical introduction to the topic, includes case studies.*

Sennett, Richard (2012), The Stupefying Smart City, lecture given on 7 Dec. 2012: opentranscripts.org/transcript/stupefying-smart-city/ (accessed: 23 Apr. 2022). *A fundamental critique of the smart city.*

The concept is driven by many influential players "who see a, if not the, central market for growth in technology-based services."[79] At the fore of this push are leaders of the global communications industry in close cooperation with some policymakers. For one, they offer new ways of organizing urban life that, furthermore, can be combined with a high profit margin. It is, therefore, no wonder that some would like to see the monetization of all of urban life. Viewed in this way, the smart city is a technology-oriented, modern variant of the *neoliberal city*. It is an effective concept because many initiatives and sometimes well-budgeted schemes are linked to the "smart" label. The EU, for example, promotes cities that want to become smart cities, as well as individual countries.

Step 3: To which question is the smart city the answer?

All in all, the limits of the concept are narrow and contradictions rampant. This is a result of its "dogmatic core, which limits its usefulness as a problem-solving tool". In the end, the concept aims to solve current and foreseeable problems through the use of new technologies. However, it was more or less ever thus – when Baron von und zum Stein was alive, when cities were electrified in the 19th century, as well as today. Stripped of its propaganda, the *smart city* can help to solve some problems, but its inner contradictions create new ones. The fact that sections of the population are left behind is generally accepted as the price of progress.

But perhaps the concept's biggest shortcoming is its reach. The *smart city* integrates and cannibalizes almost all the other concepts in this broad field. As a result, more modest but also more realistic approaches such as the *sustainable city* have little chance of being realized. Who would be willing to settle for saving resources in one city when they could save the world?

One of the greatest drivers of this concept is the economy. After the end of the *Cold War*, an economic model took precedence that, on the one hand, produced prosperity as never before but, on the other, also pushed inequality and resource consumption to new heights. This development was closely connected to cities. Which is why we need to examine an urban concept that was at the centre of these developments, that is the *neoliberal city*.

---

79   Libbe, Jens (2018), p. 437.

6. Neoliberal city

For around two generations there has been only one economic system (with only a few exceptions). Competition, growth, and profit are its guiding principles. For cities, it is no question that, as *Sebastian Schipper* has put it, "they must hold their ground in a competition to attract companies, create jobs, and ensure fiscal security and economic growth."[80]

Step 1: What kind of city is the neoliberal city?

Economic competition is the focus of attention of the concept of the *neoliberal city*, which has now been formulated in detail. Following this model, the city is organized like a corporation. "Economic competitiveness as a site for business typically takes priority over all other policy. The city engages in the production of symbolic capital, such as festivals and urban marketing, it promotes privatization and public-private partnerships, restructures the administration to mirror market-stimulating forms of governance, cuts back on social services, and increases the territorial management of marginalized groups."

Table 29. Functions of the neoliberal city

Analysis, diagnosis	Indicators, criteria	Critique	Prognosis	Ranking	Model	Vision	Objectives
–	•	•	•	•	•••	••	••

In contrast to its role during the liberal era of the 19th and 20th centuries, after the fall of socialism at the latest the state took leave of managing the economy. The logic of the market and of competition became the main steering mechanisms. That does not mean that the state has become redundant. In fact, it has set the framework for the market to increase its power. This way of thinking has inscribed itself so deeply within cities that they have become organizations in never-ending competition. This is true of almost all European and North and South American cities, as well as most Asian, African, and Russian cities. The answer to where to place the *neoliberal city* is easy. This city type is no instrument of *analysis* or *diagnosis*. *Critique* only plays a role when it attacks and, where possible, eliminates the state as entrepreneur. And so the concept acts as a *model*, often also as a *vision* with a simple *objective*. *Rankings, prognoses, indicators*, and *criteria* play a role when they underpin its orientation towards competition.

---

80   Schipper, Sebastian (2018), Neoliberale Stadt, in: Rink, Dieter; Haase, Annegret (eds.) (2018), p. 259. Also the following quotation.

My personal top 10 city websites

1) Thessaloniki, Greece
Greek
English
French

SELF-CONFIDENT: good balance of modern & classical, user-friendly & informative
thessaloniki.gr/?lang=en

2) Ulm, Germany
German
English
French

GERMANY AT ITS VERY BEST: modern & ambitious, cosmopolitan & down-to-earth
ulm.de/?ref=sharedSp&m=

3) Adelaide, Australia
English

LIKEABLE: passionate & warm, personal & communicative
cityofadelaide.com.au

4) Tel Aviv, Israel
Hebrew
English
Arabic

START-UP: Tel Aviv presents itself as a high-tech start-up; hip, innovative & full of life
tel-aviv.gov.il/Pages/HomePage.aspx

5) Montréal, Canada
English
French

INNOVATIVE HABITUS: sophisticated graphics, young, stimulating & networked
montreal.ca/en/

6) Bratislava, Slovakia
Slovak
English

ARTFUL: aesthetic, young & well-structured, with a clever English variation
bratislava.sk

7) Los Angeles, USA
English

PROFESSIONAL: service-oriented, friendly & reliable
lacity.org

8) Shanghai, China
Mandarin
English

BUSINESS TOOL: practical, down-to-earth & factual
shanghai.gov.cn

9) Bogotá, Columbia
Spanish

COMPETENT: Bogotá presents itself as a business-like service provider
bogota.gov.co

10) Riga, Latvia
Latvian
Russian

DIGITAL: Networking is the solution to everything, at least according to Riga's website
riga.lv/lv

Many thanks to Stefalina Midialkou for research support. All websites accessed: 23 Aug. 2020

Step 2: What are the features of the neoliberal city?

Like the *smart city*, the *neoliberal city* offers a panacea: the competitive economization of everyone and everything. The result, however, is a monoculture that creates many dependencies. Looking at the key features of each city, we can see that the *neoliberal city* is in no need of *unity*. Quite the contrary, the principle of all-encompassing competition does not need the city to be unified; in a way, it even runs contrary to its aim. Those who see the city as if it were a company, with its different areas making up the departments, will recognize the internal competition for recognition and resources. *Diversity* and *densification* are helpful in regard to some sectors, but the concept is most certainly not dependent on them. *Creativity* is important to modern manifestations of the *neoliberal city*, especially if a sector needs a "critical mass" to turn a profit. Without a doubt the most important feature of this city type is its *structure*. It is oriented towards entrepreneurial practices. Its credo is expansion and the optimization of everything that promotes competition, such as all types of transport links, in particular airports, classic ports, and above all the digital infrastructure.

📖 Mattissek, Annika (2018), Die neoliberale Stadt. Diskursive Repräsentationen im Stadtmarketing deutscher Großstädte. Bielefeld. *Well-grounded theoretical exploration.*

Harvey, David (2007), The Neoliberal City. youtube.com/watch?v=rfd-5kHb-Hc8 (accessed: 23 Apr. 2022). *A Marxist take on the topic.*

Hackworth, Jason (2007), The Neoliberal City. Governance, Ideology, and Development in American Urbanism. Ithaca. *Leftist take on the topic.*

Table 30. Prevalence of urban features in the neoliberal city

Conditions for action				Action
Densification	Diversity	Infrastructure	Unity	Creativity
–	–	••	–	•

Step 3: To which question is the neoliberal city the answer?

Two major developmental paths converge in the concept of the *neoliberal city*. First, it is grounded in the large group of ideas about the free market economy. After the long post-war period that was steeped in *Keynesianism* and the social market economy and as the crises began, *neoliberalism* gained the upper hand in the 1970s and 1980s. With the rise of *Thatcherism* in the United Kingdom and the opening of the financial markets – the *Big Bang* in 1986 – along with *Reaganomics* at the same time in the USA, two key national economies adopted neoliberal concepts.

Second, in the course of this development the city has become the decisive *stage* on which these concepts became manifest. It has also become both an *object* of and *platform* for this approach.

> ℹ️ *The rebound effect*
>
> This term encapsulates a number of effects that are based on the observation that increased efficiency does not lead to savings but to an increase in use or consumption. Example 1: Although the energy consumption of TVs per square inch has dropped, overall energy use by TVs has risen because screens have become larger. Example 2: Although modern automobile combustion engines use less fuel, total consumption has risen, for one because the engines have more horsepower and also because people are using their cars more often.

One clearly positive aspect is the general growth and reawakening of local economies as well as an increase in wealth. But that says nothing about the often-criticized distribution of that wealth. Many cities undeniably benefit from this concept, *London* being one of the main beneficiaries. Based on this approach, the English capital city was able to rise to become a *global city*. For other cities, however, neoliberal policies have been synonymous with decline. Lean government, the privatization and economization of numerous areas (from the labour market to culture), and the sanctioning of social inequality, to name just three aspects of neoliberalism, are not without consequential costs. Some are only now becoming apparent, such as the deterioration of vital *infrastructure* in numerous cities around the world. Recent nascent efforts at regeneration are an attempt to rectify what previous generations neglected.

All in all, the *neoliberal city* is one of the most influential concepts at the present moment. But its heyday seems to have passed; it is as helpless in the face of a pandemic as it is unable to rise to the challenge of climate change. While neoliberals claim that the free market will solve the latter problem, the facts serve to disprove their repeated assertions. All the progress that has been made in the area of environmental protection, for example, has regularly been eaten up by new growth and by the *rebound effect*. More and more people are now waking up to the fact that the challenge posed by climate change is serious. But prior to 2020, only few people were aware of another threat entirely.

7. Virus city

The danger is not visible. You can neither hear nor smell it, nor can you touch or taste it – at least not in the moment of contact. But for many people the consequences are deadly.

In December 2019, a cluster of cases of severe pneumonia was noted in the Chinese city of *Wuhan*. At first, the cause was unclear. On 30 December, the doctor *Li Wenliang* was the first to raise the suspicion of an infection with the SARS virus. Five weeks later, on 7 February 2020, he died after having been infected with the disease. The culprit was *SARS CoV-2*, the pathogen that causes the illness known as COVID-19. While medical historians will have to write the history of this pandemic, it will be years before its impact on cities will be fully understood. But at the time of writing it has already been the cause of profound changes to urban life and has led to the emergence of a new city type: the virus city.

Step 1: What kind of city is the virus city?

The all-dominant feature of this city type is the threat to the health of the entire population. *Analysis* and *diagnosis* are therefore its key features. These are based on *indicators* and *criteria* that have been predetermined by medical professionals. Since the virus was new and at the time of writing there was no vaccination, these indicators and criteria vary and we will have to break new ground when interpreting them. While *critique* plays a role, it was limited in the first weeks of the pandemic. And it mainly concerns the measures proposed by experts and implemented by politicians.

Table 31. Functions of the virus city

Analysis, diagnosis	Indicators, criteria	Critique	Prognosis	Ranking	Model	Vision	Objectives
•••	••	•	•	•	–	••	–

While there is a constant demand for *prognoses* in such cases, these are especially unreliable in pandemics. From the beginning, countries and regions created pandemic *rankings*, listing the number of people who had caught the virus, died, or recovered. We can assume that research will also create such rankings for cities. The virus city is naturally neither a *model* nor the result of set *objectives*. However, it cannot be denied that it functions as a *vision*, albeit a dystopian one.

Step 2: What are the features of the virus city?

What is key to this city type is above all the virologists' recommendations to keep social contacts to a minimum, avoiding them altogether if possible. The World Health Organization (WHO) recommends a distance of one to two metres to prevent infection via droplets. The aim of the recommendation is not to avoid the disease altogether, but to keeping transmission levels low so as to prevent public health systems collapsing. That alone points to some of the key features of the virus city.

Limiting contacts and following social distancing rules are the opposite of a lifestyle for which *densification* is a key characteristic. Without people – either temporarily or permanently – a city stops being a city. The same can be said for *diversity*. When public life is significantly reduced or even ends temporarily, there is still diversity, but it is not important. *Infrastructure* is, ultimately, limited and reduced step-by-step to what is considered essential. While one would expect *creativity* to completely dry up, there are, instead, many cases in which people met the challenges posed by the crisis together and with original ideas.

The feature that changes most in the virus city is *unity*, which appears in a new form. Crises are both levellers and divisive. On the one hand, the city again becomes more of a unit, even if it is a coming together in an emergency. The fear of getting sick or even dying, of losing one's job or needing help, as

> **Experts**
>
> Virologists such as *Melanie Brinkmann* und *Hendrik Streeck* are rarely as well-known and influential as they have become in the pandemic that began in 2019. Their recommendations are put into practice and their voices are heard, for example in public-service broadcasting podcasts. Prominent examples include the following:
>
> The "Coronavirus Update" by *Christian Drosten*, a virologist at the Charité hospital in Berlin.
>
> "Kekulés Corona Compass", a podcast by the microbiologist and biochemist *Alexander S. Kekulé* from the Martin Luther University Halle-Wittenberg.
>
> The many TV appearances by the virologist *Hendrik Streeck* from the University of Bonn.
>
> Finally, the President and Head of the Robert Koch Institute, *Lothar H. Wieler*, also became a public figure through his many appearances in live broadcasts of press conferences.

well as the experience of supply shortages and having to queue in front of supermarkets – all of that reminds people in an urban society that they are bound together by more than just place. This can be observed in ugly scenes such as panic buying as well as in unexpected acts of solidarity. While solidarity was rarely addressed at the onset of the crisis, or perhaps not even recognized, it was most certainly put into practice. "We want to protect the weak, the elderly, those with pre-existing conditions! That is why those people whose health is most at risk are not stigmatized and cut off from the rest of the population. And not even the worst autocrats ... are thinking aloud in public that a few tens of thousands of deaths might not be as bad as risking a global economic slump."[81]

This phase lasted several weeks. Then things were broken down. Economic aspects came to the fore and divided the city. As a result, urban society redefined itself.

Table 32. Prevalence of urban features in the virus city

	Conditions for action			Action
Densification	Diversity	Infrastructure	Unity	Creativity
–	–	•	••	•

Step 3: To which question is the virus city the answer?

Nobody planned the virus city and only few people predicted it. It arose as the consequence of a global pandemic and within days turned on their head things that had been taken for granted for decades. The key impacts on the city were:

- Basic rights were restricted and urban citizens became the occupants, patients, perhaps even prisoners in a giant infirmary.
- Alliances that had been built up over decades collapsed, for example the EU in the second week of March 2020 when some countries panicked and closed their borders without even informing the EU of this step. Borders that

---

81 di Lorenzo, Giovanni, commentary in *DIE ZEIT*, 19 March 2020.

seemed to have disappeared long ago reappeared and freedom of movement was restricted, or even ended.
- The economy lost the gains it had made over more than a decade. Global supply chains were suddenly unreliable and the dependencies they cause called into question. Jobs were lost or put at risk. Unemployment was felt first by people in precarious jobs, the self-employed, and small companies; larger companies were able to hold out a little longer. Stock markets nosedived.
- A rule of expertise was established. Since viruses are a specialized field, in the spring of 2020 neither the economic, political, nor societal sectors were able to make informed decisions. They were dependent on the knowledge and advice of experts. Almost everywhere, this knowledge and advice was turned straight into practical policy. Never before had cities been so dependent on scientific expertise. Where expert advice was not followed or the existence of the pandemic even denied, the impact was worse and the number of deaths higher. New York City was one of the most dramatic cases.
- The urban lifestyle died and hit the new middle class – which we will look at more closely in IV.C.3 "Society and the economy" – hardest.

The *virus city* is the answer to an existential crisis. It is the opposite of the *open city*. It does away with a core feature of the city, namely density. It is too early to say how exactly this new city type will affect other terms, concepts, and city types. But there will be consequences to be sure. Temporarily at least, the *global city*, the *arrival city*, and the *neoliberal city* have become less important in a world that is shutting itself in, and the *capital city* has regained its importance as a crisis management centre.

It is even possible that urban life will never again be as it was before the pandemic. While authoritarian states are using the virus as an excuse to consolidate and expand their power, democracies want to lift all the restrictions imposed. But wanting may not be enough. If the virus remains for years, then the following may be possible: "Since the threat of infectious disease, like the threat of terrorism, never goes away, control measures can easily become permanent." It is difficult to predict what the crisis will mean for cities in the long term. But events like this most certainly have the capacity to become existential threats. In the worst case, it is possible that the global globalization trend will be reversed and cities will begin to shrink – or even disappear altogether.

8. Shrinking city and lost city

From a neoliberal perspective, there is an easy answer to the question of why cities shrink in "normal" times: a *shrinking city* has simply lost the global competition. Liberalism holds both opportunities and risks. The shrinking city did not make the most of the opportunities it was given. This answer makes it clear how much our view has over the past decades become restricted to the economy.

> **Waves of urban shrinkage**
>
> 1) The first wave of shrinking cities was a result of *suburbanization*. It began in the 19th century with the *garden city* movement. Suburbs grew in number in the USA and Europe because more people owned cars after World War II, and they continue to be dominant today.
>
> 2) A second wave came with the demise of the traditional coal and steel centres starting in the 1970s. Cities in the *Ruhr region* in Germany or *Liverpool* in the United Kingdom (that had one of the longest periods of shrinking ever observed, from the 1930s to the 2000s) are prominent examples, as are steel towns in the East and Midwest of the USA or *Detroit*, the "Motor City".
>
> 3) A third wave followed after the end of the Cold War. Many people in Eastern Europe used their newly-found freedom of movement to seek opportunities in the West, and in the early 21st century three quarters of large Eastern European and Russian cities began to shrink. Not one business sector remained competitive in the face of the introduction of capitalism.

Step 1: What kind of city is the shrinking city?

Shrinking cities and *lost cities* are not a new phenomenon. They have existed throughout human history. *Pompeii*, buried under a layer of ash following the eruption of Vesuvius in 79 CE, is the best-known but by no means only example from *antiquity*. In more recent times, wars such as World War II have been the main cause of urban shrinkage. But even cities that were completely laid to waste, such as *Hiroshima* and *Nagasaki* in Japan after atomic bombs were dropped on them in 1945, have been rebuilt.

Cities are comparatively rarely lost entirely. It is more common for them to shrink, although there is no universal definition of the term. It always denotes a falling population, everything else boils down to discussions of cause and effect. One-dimensional interpretations make it difficult to assess the phenomenon. For example because the spatial aspect is also important. If a city centre becomes less densely populated as a result of suburbanization, and at the same time the surrounding area becomes more populated, that is not necessarily a crisis. Every case needs to be examined in its own right.

When placing this city type in context, it quickly becomes clear that we are looking almost exclusively at *analysis* and *diagnosis*. Indicators and *criteria* revolve mostly around population, more exactly around its decrease. The other areas are not affected, or only indirectly. We cannot completely ignore the importance of setting objectives, however, since there are some schemes for redesigning *shrinking cities* for the future.

Table 33. Functions of the shrinking city

Analysis, diagnosis	Indicators, criteria	Critique	Prognosis	Ranking	Model	Vision	Objectives
•••	•	–	–	–	–	–	–

Step 2: What are the features of the shrinking city?

The main characteristic of a shrinking city – a decline in population – has already been mentioned. The question remains as to the cause, whereby industrial transformation and the loss of jobs are currently the most common. Cities that are dependent on one industry, such as *coal mining towns*, are particularly vulnerable. Other causes are *suburbanization* and demographic change, particularly in an ageing population. Weather events such as storms and floods are becoming more important factors. Examples include the "Great Hurricane" of 1870, the deadliest storm to date with a death toll of between 22,000 and 27,000 people. The next large storms were Hurricane Mitch (1998), which caused over 11,000 deaths and Hurricane Fifi (1974) with between 8,000 and 10,000 deaths. In monetary terms, the worst were Harvey in 2017 and Katrina in 2005, the most expensive storms to date, each with consequential costs of 125 billion US dollars, followed by Maria (2017), which cost 91.6 billion US dollars.

Table 34. Prevalence of urban features in the shrinking city

Conditions for action				Action
Densification	Diversity	Infrastructure	Unity	Creativity
–	–	•	–	–

The devastation caused by Hurricane Katrina, which almost completely flooded the city of *New Orleans*, is etched in recent memory. Before the storm, the city had a population of almost half a million. During the storm, New Orleans was evacuated and one year later the city's population had been cut in half. People only slowly returned. In 2019, the population was around 390,000.

When we consider the key urban features, we can see that they are either weak or non-existent. *Densification* decreases, *unity* falls apart, there is less *diversity*, and also less *creativity*. Only the *structure*, or what is left of it, remains for a time. When cities are able to recover, the infrastructure provides the backbone for their restructuring.

All of the above is also true of *lost cities* – only to a more catastrophic extent. Cities that are lost have no structure at all, only some artifacts and people's memories, and sometimes only the latter.

Step 3: To which question is the shrinking city the answer?

Shrinking and *lost cities* are almost always regarded as being in crisis. This is generally regarded as a negative process in which, for example, those that cannot stand up to the competition for growth are scaled down and shrink. The consequences are vacant housing, abandoned city centre areas, debt and dire finances, loss of jobs, an ageing population, brain drain, and more. Looked at it that way, *shrinking cities* are not the answer to a question, but the consequence of an economic model that promises success, which means it also produces losers.

Detroit is one of the most unusual cases of this city type. In 1950, almost 1.85 million people lived in the city centre. By 2017, only around one third of them (673,000) were left. In June 2009, the city's biggest employer, General Motors, went into liquidation, which was followed by its unprecedented demise

📖 Lampen, Angelika; Owzar, Armin (eds.) (2008), Schrumpfende Städte. Ein Phänomen zwischen Antike und Moderne. Cologne. *Basic introduction and good overview.*

Richardson, Henry W.; Nam, Chang Woon (eds.) (2014), Shrinking Cities. New York. *Comprehensive anthology.*

Oswalt, Philipp (ed.) (2005), Schrumpfende Städte. Vol. 1 and Vol. 2. Berlin. *Anthologies of international comparisons.*

and ended in the city going bankrupt in July 2013. Thousands of apartments were left empty, one third of the urban area was abandoned, and criminality was rampant.

But since the mid-2010s, there have been signs of rejuvenation. Like *Berlin* in the early 1990s, the ailing city lured creative young people who needed space to try out their ideas. Galleries, ateliers, and clubs began to pop up. Some areas have become attractive, such as the almost completely rebuilt Eastern Market area, and some parts of Downtown and of Motown. Droves of young people are moving into the city and developing a new lifestyle. Particularly interesting, and almost revolutionary for the USA, is the value placed on good food. Detroit is now known as home to some of the best cocktail bars and restaurants in the country. Alongside the ubiquitous fast-food chains, a modern, young, and innovative foody scene has taken root that serves regional products that are often grown within the city limits. "Made in Detroit" no longer stands for American cars, but for good food produced in the city itself.

Figure 10. Downtown Detroit, 2010.

It is too early to say whether this development will have long-term success. At the moment, it appears unimaginable that it will come anywhere close to balancing out the losses of recent decades. Nevertheless, crisis really does breed opportunity. Having lost the usual growth race, Detroit had no other choice but to start again and to foster new ideas and start-ups. Detroit is remarkable in that it is thus one of the first metropolises to forge a new path in this way.

9. Terms, concepts, and city types: valuable patterns?

The method

There are hundreds of different city types. But the sample chosen in the above already reveals certain patterns. To recapitulate, the idea of city types goes back to *Max Weber*'s idea of the ideal type. His aim was to find concepts that are distinct enough to help him order and understand the phenomena he had discovered. To do that, he isolated the characteristics he was interested in and found meaningful and logical connections between them.

The advantage of this method is that it reduces our complex reality to such an extent as to give it clearer contours and make it easier to grasp. The risk in reducing reality to the most interesting phenomena in this way makes us lose sight of the rest. The more clearly a city type is delineated – the *global city* and the *neoliberal city* are prime examples – the more other parts of the city are ignored.

No city type describes the urban area as a whole, only elements of it. The *virus city*, the *shrinking city*, and the *lost city* are extreme examples of this. And it is unusual for any attempt to be made to clarify the relationship between the part, or sometimes parts, of the city that are described and the rest of the city. Exceptions to this rule among the works we have looked at include *Richard Sennett's open city* (III.B.9) and *Doug Saunders's arrival city* (IV.B.4).

That leads us to ask what exactly is being described? An issue and its impact on the city? Or a city and its relevance for the issue? At best, the answer is both and their interdependencies; as a rule, however, it is only the former. Because of this, what a city is, at its core, is quite blurred.

Creating city types has one other effect that has to do with one of the basic instruments that is used in the social sciences. While natural scientists can conduct *experiments* to test their theses, social scientists are dependent on *comparisons*. But it is difficult to compare different city types, because they were created by people working in different fields, with methods that are inherent to their own discipline and following the logic of the issue that interests them. Thus, descriptions have been provided that are coherent in themselves, but their relationship to one another remains unclear. There is no way of assessing whether, for example, the *smart city* is a more promising approach than the *sustainable city* – although these two city types are still relatively close.

To make headway, the examples chosen were analysed only as far as necessary in order to be able to answer three questions about them. First, we asked about their *function*. There is a difference between a term, a concept, or city type being developed to help understand a particular development or to formulate a vision.

The second question concerns the prevalence of the features that characterize each city type (as described in III.C.13).

In the third step, we took the question that *Hans J. Nissen* developed for his study of the origins of cities and adapted it for application to the present. This question is: To which question is each city type the answer? What problem does it solve?

The aim of this three-part operation is, on the one hand, simply to recognize that people had very different motives for developing the various terms, concepts, and city types, and they are the way they are. We asked the above questions so that we could nevertheless evaluate them all.

A comparison of the functions of the various city types

The *Handbuch der Stadtkonzepte* (Manual of Urban Concepts) makes the most convincing suggestion in terms of the first question regarding where to place the various city types. The authors ask what the function of different city types is and analyse a total of 21 cases.[82] Based on the types looked at more closely, it is possible to come to some preliminary conclusions.

1) First, the intuitive assumption is correct: cities always fulfill more than one function. Even prominent cities are always multifunctional, never monofunctional. When that no longer holds true, we can no longer speak of a "city", as the borderline cases show.
2) Within this multifunctionality we can make out areas in which certain city types are stronger or weaker. Analytical city types in particular, such as the *global city*, the *arrival city*, or the *shrinking city*, focus on specific phenomena, in these cases the global economy, worldwide migration, and urban decline, respectively. These city types are grounded in the present, but if we regard them as the result of a development, then the past naturally also plays a role.

Other city types have other functions. They are constructed in order to shape the future. The past interests them only because it serves as a contrast. Examples include, in particular, the *smart city* as a *vision*, and the *neoliberal city* as a *model*. It is no coincidence that the corresponding *objectives* can be derived from both.

Table 35. Analysis of functions of the various city types

Function/City type	Analysis, diagnosis	Indicators, criteria	Critique	Prognosis	Ranking	Model	Vision	Objectives
Megacity	•••	–	•	••	–	–	–	–
Global city	•••	••	–	•	•••	••	•	••
Capital city	–	••	•	•	–	••	•	••
Arrival city	•••	–	••	•	–	••	–	–
Smart city	•	–	•	–	••	••	•••	••
Neoliberal city	–	•	•	•	•	•••	••	••
Virus city	•••	••	•	•	•	–	••	–
Shrinking | Lost city	•••	•	–	–	–	–	–	–

---

82 Rink, Dieter; Haase, Annegret (eds.) (2018). Strictly speaking, there are actually 10 functions. Combining *analysis*, i.e. the examination of a topic's constitutive elements, and *diagnosis*, a summary evaluation, is quite problematic. The terms are quite similar, but not identical; they serve each other and there are overlaps, as is the case for *indicators* and *criteria*. Furthermore, the terms *objectives*, *model*, and *vision* are all variations on thinking into the future, and there are no clear boundaries. Although the definitions of these function could be subject to criticism, I follow the suggestion put forward in the manual.

The first group refers to the city as it is (empiricism) and the second provides a picture of what it should be (idea). While we are on solid ground in the former categories, the latter are rife with ideologies and marketing. This first evaluation therefore provides a grid that helps us see more clearly where a city type sits.

A comparison of the features of the various city types

To hone in more closely, we can look at the features of the different types of cities. In the theory section, we determined the five main features of a city: *densification, diversity, structure, unity,* and *creativity*. These are comprised of both the conditions needed for action within a city as well as the action itself. But that says nothing about the prevalence of these features. That is the next question we asked. In summary, we find that:

1) As far as the four conditions for urban agency are concerned, we find that *infrastructure* is present, important, or dominant in all the city types we analysed. Nothing works without infrastructure, not even in the marginal cases of the *virus city* or the *shrinking city*, and even in the *lost city* it, or at least parts of it, are the last thing that remains.
2) *Densification*, although it is a dominant feature in terms of providing the framework for acting within a city, plays only a small role in the examples chosen, which is due to the types selected. But when densification is reduced, as in the outlier cases, the city ceases to be a city.
3) When it comes to *diversity*, only the *neoliberal city* can do without, otherwise it is always present and, in the case of the *arrival city*, extremely important.
4) *Unity* is key to the *capital city*, the *arrival city*, and the *virus city*; it is irrelevant for the other city types.
5) Human agency, to which we attributed *creative action*, is, like *densification*, present in almost all city types. All the examples studied (with the exception of the borderline cases) agree that people act in a certain way, even though the action itself takes place in different areas.

Table 36. Prevalence of urban features in the various city types

| | FEATURES that… | | | | |
| | ...set the conditions for action in the city | | | | ...describe the acts performed within the city |
CITY TYPE	Densification	Diversity	Infrastructure	Unity	Creativity
Megacity	•••	••	•	–	••
Global city	•	•	•••	–	•••
Capital city	•	•	•••	••	•••
Arrival city	••	•••	•	••	••
Smart city	–	•	••	–	••
Neoliberal city	–	–	••	–	•
Virus city	–	–	•	••	•
Shrinking | Lost city	–	–	•	–	–

In III.C.3 we argued that the five features mentioned here are found in every city and even define it. But in the above comparison there are cases in which some features do not show up at all. That has nothing to do with the fact that they do not exist in reality, but with the question of how important the individual features are for a particular city type. Those cases in which individual features play no role at all are, therefore, striking. One thing that stands out is that more than half of the city types analysed are, ultimately, not interested in *unity*. They either ignore the division of urban society, accept it as a necessary evil, or even promote it. The question remains for urbanists as to whether they should continue to advance such concepts and accept the consequences, or rather treat them as a problem that needs to be dealt with.

In sum, looking at the prevalence of urban features in different city types gives us information on the direction in which each kind of city is headed, regardless of whether this was an organic or a planned development. Taken together with the functions analysed in the above, we can now assess different city types according to the aims they serve and also according to how prevalent the features that are typical of that city type are or are supposed to be.

Cities' specializations

City types reflect the different areas in which cities specialize. Cities face a multitude of challenges: growth through migration, global economic developments, the need to administer territories, mitigating the effects of climate change or pandemics, the risks of competitive business practices. If we turn these challenges into questions, the different city types can be read as answers to them.

This allows us to know 1) what we are dealing with, for example an *analysis* and *diagnosis* or a *vision*, to name the opposite ends of the spectrum and 2) which features of the city types are important and which they disregard or do not value. With this information we can 3) formulate the question to which the city type is an answer.

Different city types attach different weight to certain issues and are, in practice, used to manage resources. That is why it is important to look at city types, because they explain both the interests linked to these ideas and the heated debates within and between the academic disciplines. What is at stake is who controls the narrative. And money. How this money is distributed is in large part determined by the issues the city has to cope with. They are the subject of the final chapter.

Table 37. To which question is each city type the answer?

QUESTION	ANSWER	CITY TYPE
How can a city cope with the increase in global migration?	By growing	Megacity
	By actively shaping this development	Arrival city
How can complex territories be managed?	Though highly specialized command centres	Capital city
How is the global economy managed?		Global city
How can a city win the economic competition?	By transforming the city into a business	Neoliberal city
How can the urban population be protected against an epidemic or pandemic?	By reducing human contact; by reducing population density, a key feature of the city	Virus city
How high are the competitive risks?	Those that cannot stand up to the competition leave the path of growth and shrink or even disappear	Shrinking | Lost city
How can the conflicting aims of classic economics and environmental protection be reconciled?	By linking and harmonizing the two principles	Smart city

C. Urban issues

Different terms, concepts, and city types prioritize different issues. Depending on how finely they are distinguished, there may be one to two dozen key issues that are relevant for cities. Almost all of them are interlinked, overlap, and influence each other. In the name of brevity, we can only examine a few of these issues. The selection has been made by looking at which topics are currently being discussed most intensively and controversially on the global level; closely connected issues are addressed together. Each section begins with facts relating to the status quo, followed by a discussion of important consequences for the city and possible future outcomes. Since the most pressing issue is dealt with at the end of this chapter, we will begin with the second most important concern of our times, that is immigration and emigration.

1. Immigration and emigration

Percentage of city dwellers born in other countries

Dubai	83%
Brussels	62%
Toronto	46%
Auckland, Sydney, Los Angeles	39%
Singapore	38%
London, New York City	37%
Melbourne	35%
Amsterdam	28%
Frankfurt am Main	37%
Paris	25%

Worldwide, 37,000 people per day and 70.8 million people per year are forcibly displaced as a result of persecution and war.[83] A total of around 250 million people around the world are migrants. Internal *migration* is almost three times as high: around 763 million people live outside the region in which they were born. Taken together, that is 1.04 billion people, or 13.4 per cent of the global population.

In the main, these people find temporary or permanent homes in cities that already have large populations. In the USA, the United Kingdom, Canada, and Australia, over 90 per cent of new immigrants settle in urban areas.

Migration is one of the largest drivers of urbanization. As we have seen by comparing *Doug Saunders's Arrival City* with *Mike Davis*'s *Planet of Slums* (IV.B.4.), these processes and their impact can be examined from very different perspectives. From here, many developmental paths are possible:

1) Cities continue to grow. They need to offer protection and living and working opportunities to the people who have moved there temporarily or permanently.
2) One feature of migration is that most migrants who move to new cities settle on the fringes and not in the city centre.
3) As a result, new cultures arise, often creating enclaves and so-called *parallel societies*. The diversity of religions, languages, ethnicities, and cultures

---

[83] unhcr.org/dach/de/services/statistiken (accessed: 23 Apr. 2020). The following statistics are also taken from this source.

that enter a city through migration can both enrich urban life and threaten social cohesion, traditional cultures, and security. Social tension, xenophobia, discrimination, and even violence can be seen in neighbourhoods, workplaces, or in schools. Since such cases tend to garner a great deal of attention, positive aspects are often overlooked. That distorts the bigger picture, for positive impacts are in fact more common.[84]

 Best – Worst

Figure 11

There is no lack of negative perspectives on migration, which is why I would like to mention one particularly encouraging project: *Cities of Migration*. Its website (*citiesofmigration.ca*) is a treasure trove of best practice examples.

4) In economic terms, migrants contribute around 10 per cent to global gross domestic product (GDP). Most migrants are eager to work so they can integrate into the new society and improve their own lives.
5) It is not national governments but local governments that are both directly affected and often responsible for migrants. Migration can put pressure on *infrastructure* that is often already insufficient and means urban society needs to be redefined.
6) Urban areas are transformed whether or not these processes are actively managed. Transnational migration and the concurrent global connections between individuals, companies, and cultures has turned many cities into global centres, for example *Dubai*, *Kuala Lumpur*, *London*, *New York*, *Sydney*, and *Toronto*.
7) A further impact of migration is a change in political culture, especially in liberal democracies. A part of society feels sidelined and threatened by migration. While migration can bring changes, these fears are often most pronounced in regions and countries that have little or no immigration. The issue is particularly good ammunition for populist movements in places with no practical experience, a development, analysed in detail by the political scientists *Ivan Krastev* and *Stephen Holmes* in their book *The Light that Failed*, which can be seen, for example, in the politics of *Donald Trump* in the *USA*, *Viktor Mihály Orbán* in *Hungary*, the *PiS party* in *Poland*, and the *AfD* in *Germany*.[85]

These are some of the most important consequences that migration has for cities. They hold true for both migration within and between countries and are exacerbated by environmental destruction through pollution, destabilization, and natural disasters. They are forcing more and more people to leave their homes. In 2016, the number of climate migrants was estimated to be around 24 mil-

---

84 www3.weforum.org/docs/Migration_Impact_Cities_report_2017_low.pdf (accessed: 23 Apr. 2022).
85 iom.int/global-compact-migration (accessed: 23 Apr. 2022). See, for example, Ionesco, Diana; Mokhnacheva, Daria; Gemenne, François (2017), The Atlas of Environmental Migration. New York.

lion.[86] According to forecasts, this number will soon rise to anywhere between 50 and 150 million people. This goes hand in hand with two other phenomena: rural flight and the disappearance of villages (IV.C.6.) as well as shrinking cities.

In a nutshell, it can be said that on account of the scope and complexity of migration, it will remain one of the most important issues to impact urban life for many years to come. If we are going to look more closely at urban life, we need to examine more closely how and where people live in cities.

2. Housing and living

The housing options in cities are as wide-ranging as human possibilities: from a sleeping bag in front of the *Public Library* in downtown *Los Angeles* to a loft worth millions in the *Burj Khalifa* in *Dubai* that stands at 829.8 metres tall. While the size, quality, type, and form of real estate, that is immoveable property, constantly changes, the basic model has remained the same for thousands of years. With minimal refurbishment apartments and houses dating back to antiquity that are in a decent condition could be lived in today.

Housing has become a problem almost all over the world for people who live in cities; space is limited, demand is higher than supply, and prices are high. Exceptions such as the housing market in *shrinking cities* are the exception that proves this rule. Prices are a particular problem in prospering metropolises. Only the *upper classes* have enough resources to buy or rent something in the quality they desire. The *middle classes* (a poorly-defined term that we will examine more closely in the next section) increasingly find themselves in a critical situation. Often, they do not earn enough to pay for housing with enough space for two or more people, so that they have to make do with poorer-quality housing in less desirable locations. Cities that react to this problem with housing programmes outside of the city centre help reduce the pressure but also create new problems, such as increased traffic volume or the emergence of enclaves. The *lower classes* suffer most, since they can only afford basic housing, and often none at all. The causes are many and interlinked. Two are particularly influential:

For one, real estate is one of the largest business sectors worldwide. In Germany alone, gross fixed assets from real estate stood at around 17.3 billion euros in 2016.[87] Most municipalities have pulled back from social housing schemes over the past 30 years, a trend that is now slowly being reversed in some places. For the time being, urban living is above all a question of price.

But there is also an issue of displacement as younger and wealthier classes take over the living quarters of long-established residents.

Living and housing are closely linked. Just how closely can be seen in the famous early 20th-century quote by the Berlin artist *Heinrich Zille*: "You can kill a person with an apartment just as well as with an axe." That is still true, par-

---

86 www.umweltbundesamt.de/sites/default/files/medien/5750/publikationen/2021-05-19_texte_79-2021_migration.pdf (accessed: 23 Apr. 2022).
87 en.wikipedia.org/wiki/Real_estate_economics (accessed: 23 Apr. 2022).

ticularly in the cities of the Global South. Equally as important as housing is the neighbourhood it is in, and its stores and public facilities. Here, too, the amount of money residents have plays a key role. Money is also linked to, but does not alone determine, lifestyle. Lifestyle and financial means influence each other and have, for around a generation, also been connected to *globalization*, which, in turn, has an impact on individual neighbourhoods and entire cities.

This process, known as "*gentrification*", has no precise scientific definition. Usually, the word is used as a political slogan. A good overview of the current situation is provided in the *Handbook of Gentrification Studies*.[88]

Numerous lists rank cities according to "liveability". In 2018, the *Economist*'s popular list ranked *Vienna*, *Melbourne*, and *Sydney* at the top and *Damascus*, *Lagos*, and *Dhaka* at the bottom.[89] Other lists have similar rankings. These lists have a two-fold influence. They have a *direct* impact by increasing demand on the hous-

 *Best – Worst*

Chile – Constitución: In February 2010, a massive earthquake killed over 500 people and made thousands homeless. The Chilean architect *Alejandro Aravena* and his team are not specialized in luxury real estate, but in affordable, high-quality social housing. He had the idea of building unfinished houses that the owners could themselves complete according to their needs.

Figures 12–13

Germany – Kreuzberg, Berlin city centre: Designed as a model housing development, the hopes attached to the New Kreuzberg Centre – a 1974 example of social housing and urban development – were quickly dashed and the project became one of the biggest disappointments of the second half of the 20th century. The complex and its environs – the infamous Kottbusser Tor area – became a slum. It was not until Berlin's "soft" urban renewal programme of the 1980s, and the *Quartiersmanagement* system of neighbourhood centres instituted in 1999 to promote integration in low-income areas, that revitalization was successful.

ing market in the top-ranked cities and an *indirect* impact because they make these cities more attractive tourist destinations. Both, in turn, drive *gentrification*. They also encourage another phenomenon that is linked to modern mass tourism: the number of apartments rented to tourists has increased to such an extent that some neighbourhoods, even entire city centres, have been revamped to accommodate a new, individualist event culture. Locals both profit and suffer from this development.

This changed drastically with the advent of the global pandemic in 2019. From March 2020, the tourism industry went into global stillstand. It is too early to be able to assess the long-term impact.

Housing and living are causally linked to massive social transformations. These, in turn, are linked to shifts in the economy and the labour market. And so that is what we will turn to in the next section.

---

88   Lees, Loretta; Phillips, Martin (eds.) (2019), Handbook of Gentrification Studies. Cheltenham.
89   eiu.com/n/the-global-liveability-index-2019/ (accessed: 23 Apr. 2022).

3. Society and the economy

In the 1980s, there was no way of foreseeing the social revolution that has transformed the world since the turn of the century. The sociologist *Ulrich Beck* – and many others besides – instead saw a path towards "a mobile society, beyond class and rank". Instead, while individualization did grow worldwide, "cultural lifestyles [are] not equal. Rather they vary as to their opportunities, their life experiences, and their social prestige."[90]

The envisaged pluralism proved to be an illusion. Instead, conflicts erupted, replacing what *Helmut Schelsky* called the "levelled middle-class society", referring to Germany in the 1950s. The sociologist *Andreas Reckwitz* calls it a *new class society* consisting of an "upwardly-mobile, highly-qualified new middle class of academics, a stagnating old or traditional middle class, and a new downwardly-mobile underclass or precarious class." In addition, there is a small upper class of the uber-rich. This class dynamic creates a "turnstile society": while the new middle class outgrows the old, the lower class drops out of it.

This development has also replaced historical differences between industrial and developing countries. Class struggle is now determined less by material capital and more by social and cultural capital. That makes developments impossible to compare, even if much of the vocabulary of the historical class struggle remains the same. This new view of society does not replace the concept of different *milieus* that has become widely accepted in past decades. Milieus continue to exist, but they are insufficient to explain contemporary conflicts. It is only by superimposing both analyses that milieus can be matched with classes.

These social transformations lead to shifts in urban housing and labour markets. The main driver is the emergence of a new type of economy that can be seen as the current apex of a three-tiered development: "… a long phase of parallel static agricultural economy and mercantile capitalism, a second phase of industrial modernity and finally the third and current phase of post-industrial, cognitive and cultural capitalism."

Statistics bear out this development: In the 1960s and 1970s, around half of all workers were employed in traditional industrial production. That number has fallen by half. At the same time, the number of employees in the service sector has risen by around 75 per cent. This has gone hand in hand with a revolution in consumer habits. After basic needs have been met, in the middle classes in particular demand has risen for goods "from which consumers expect cultural value and cultural uniqueness, from adventure travel to Netflix series, from designer clothing to an organic diet and an apartment in an exclusive location."

Urban labour markets have changed accordingly. The number of jobs is increasing that produce that added value – and those neighbourhoods whose offices, apartments, stores, and restaurants embody this lifestyle are "in". The

---

90 Reckwitz, Andreas (2019), Das Ende der Illusionen. Politik, Ökonomie und Kultur in der Spätmoderne. Berlin, p. 63. The following quotations: p. 67, p. 143, and p. 141.

result is a new animosity between the new and the old middle classes, and the new middle classes and the lower classes.

This development is also mirrored in the transportation sector. While the new middle classes engage in passionate discussions about alternatives, and test them out, the global trend is moving in another direction.

> 🛈 **The new class society**
>
> Characteristics of the new classes:
> 1) *The traditional middle class:* settled, orderly, and culturally defensive
> 2) *The new middle class:* successful, self-fulfilment, urban cosmopolitanism, upwardly-mobile
> 3) *The precarious class:* dropped out of the middle class, hand-to-mouth existence, at risk of further downward mobility

4. Movement and standstill

The number of automotive vehicles in the world reached 1.2 billion in 2015. This development has been breathtaking. In 1930, there were 35 million vehicles in the entire world. By 1950, that number had risen to 70 million, by 1970 to 250 million, and by 1990 to 280 million. In 2010, the one billion threshold was crossed.[91] One form of transportation has conquered the earth – and its cities. Even without looking at the distribution of vehicles, its impact is wide-ranging. Three consequences are briefly sketched below.

1) Today's urban world is an automotive world. The automobile, with its promise of independence and mobility, remains the number one means of transportation. And cities were redesigned in the 20th century to become more *car-friendly*. Since the mid-20th century, this development has asserted itself as a lifestyle that transcends all political ideologies.
2) As the traffic congestion index shows, this form of mobility has entered partial standstill. The index is an analysis of the navigation data of 416 cities, undertaken in 2019. The extra time it takes to drive a certain distance was calculated as a percentage and the cities were ranked accordingly. The most congested cities were *Bengaluru* and *Manila* (both +71%) and *Bogotá* (+68%). But even in the cities at the bottom of the list, *Akron*, *Cádiz* (both −10%), and *Greensboro-High Point* (+9%), drivers contended with 10 and 9 per cent additional time, respectively.
   While congestion is the result of high traffic density, the pandemic led to a completely different kind of standstill. Lockdowns led to a significant decrease in and, in some cases, to a complete standstill of urban traffic.
3) The biggest problem that transportation causes is environmental pollution, since almost all vehicles are driven by combustion engines. Emission-free alternatives at local level, such as electric cars, made up only 0.5% of all cars in 2020. Global emissions from transportation stood at around 18 per cent at the time of writing.[92]

---

91 On congestion, see tomtom.com/en_gb/traffic-index/ (accessed: 23 Apr. 2022).
92 de.statista.com/statistik/daten/studie/317683/umfrage/verkehrsttraeger-anteil-co2-emissionenfossile-brennstoffe/ (accessed: 23 Apr. 2022).

> ⓘ Best – Worst
>
> *Medellín, Columbia:* In 2004, the city opened its first municipal cable car line. Two lines now connect poor neighbourhoods to the public transportation network. Half a million residents' commute has thus been cut in half. The measure also boosted social and economic integration in these neighbourhoods. One result has been a drop in criminal activity and an increase in the number of local businesses.
>
> *Bangalore, India:* Nobody spends more time in traffic jams than drivers in Bangalore: in 2019 an average of 243 hours.

These facts make it clear that there is a conflict between the need for individual mobility and the desire for an urban lifestyle that is *not* dominated by traffic and its consequences, not to mention climate-friendly. Slowly, the problem is being noticed, and concepts such as the *sustainable city* or the *smart city* are first attempts to find solutions. One positive example is *Hong Kong*, which, with a population of seven million in a small area, is one of the most densely settled regions in the world. Only around 1 per cent of Hong Kong residents own a car, the public transport network is extensive, and the average daily commute is just over half an hour. Other model cities are *Stockholm* and *Amsterdam*, which boast an extensive and well-used network of bicycle paths.[93]

Despite basic agreement on the fact that automobile traffic needs to decrease in urban areas and public transport needs to increase, the forecasts predict the opposite. Some researchers believe that the number of cars in the world will double by 2040.

These issues are linked to big economic questions. On the one hand, there is the desire for environmentally-friendly mobility in urban areas, which requires enormous investments. On the other hand, there is the automobile industry with its global sales of over 3.3 billion US dollars and its interest in increasing its profits. It is unclear how this conflict of interests, with its far-reaching consequences for cities, can be resolved.

However, the current debate revolves around other issues, in particular new forms of urban mobility. What is under discussion, and in places also being put into practice, is the expansion of public transportation networks and bicycle paths, park and ride facilities, car sharing, e-scooters, and much more. Specialization and exemplary solutions can be observed. *Amsterdam, Copenhagen, Utrecht, Barcelona,* and *Portland,* for example, have become *bicycle cities*. They have an extensive infrastructure with bike paths, including bicycle highways, and bicycle garages etc. This infrastructure has led to a marked increase in the number of cyclists, and in some places bicycles now make up over 50 per cent of city centre traffic. While such positive examples exist, globally they are few and far between – and they also cannot solve all problems for everyone in every city. It is too early to say which solutions will prevail in the long run in which cities. But it is safe to say that a new diversification of vehicles is supplanting, or at least supplementing, the monoculture of automobiles.

---

93 See the *Copenhagenize Index,* which measures efforts to establish bicycles as a form of transportation (copenhagenizeindex.eu). Its 13 criteria are useful mostly for urban planners; cyclists are better informed by the *bike-friendly cities ranking*: fahrradklima-test.adfc.de/english (accessed: 23 Apr. 2022).

5. Analogue and digital

The internet is the most influential technology of the present. Within one generation, it has become a global and universal tool.

In 2020, almost four billion people, or around 60 per cent of the global population, used the *World Wide Web*. But the digital transformation is even more pervasive and far-reaching than these statistics suggest. It has an almost infinite number of uses in all areas and permeates all areas of life. While earlier industrial revolutions first changed the world of work and then, as a consequence, people's private lives, the digital transformation is turning both on their heads at a previously unknown speed. But there is another way in which the digital transformation is different from all other technological revolutions. Applications produce more data than they need to do what they must. Navigation tools in cars, for example, provide information on how many vehicles are on a particular route and inform users, without their being asked, whether there is a threat of congestion and that a different route might save time. Smartwatches recommend walking more to reach a health-promoting daily steps goal.

"What problem does digitalization solve?"[94] The radical consequence of digitalization is, on the one hand, that applications produce an added value that users do not actually need them for and, on the other hand, that they offer solutions for things that nobody even thought presented a problem. Nevertheless, it remains true to say that "if it works, technology will prevail".

The digital transformation is creating a whole new realm of possibilities for cities. Large portions of urban *infrastructure*, transportation, and administrative systems are already being managed, either completely or partially, by computers, making them more efficient. For users, all types of municipal services are now also easier to access. And recent urban concepts such as the *smart city* (IV.B.5) put the digital transformation at the centre of their vision for urban areas. The two main arguments for using digital solutions in cities are 1) *efficiency*, because a considerable number of administrative tasks can be done better and faster, and 2) *opportunities*, because connecting various areas creates opportunities that did not previously exist.

Expectations were high during the peak stage of the digital transformation. The tech magazine with the punk habitus *WIRED*, for example, wrote in the spring of 2000 about the USA: "We are, as a nation, better educated, more tolerant, and more connected because of – not in spite of – the convergence of the Internet and public life."[95] Hardly a decade later, that has proved to be perhaps the biggest lie of the internet community. Yet that is no reason for a Luddite revolution, but rather for a sober reckoning.

---

94 A question raised by the sociologist Nassehi, Armin (2019), Muster. Theorie der digitalen Gesellschaft. Munich, p. 12. The following quotation: p. 326.
95 Cited in Lepore, Jill (2019), These Truths: A History of the United States. New York, p. 730.

> **Problems of the digital transformation**
>
> 1) Digital security is limited. Administrative networks are large and make use of different hardware and software. That makes them vulnerable.
> 2) For a time, computerization means that routine processes (electronic filing systems) create more, or even double, the amount of work. That is hardly trivial for municipal administrations.
> 3) The digital transformation creates dependencies. Eight of the 10 largest providers are in the USA. China has created its own market and Russia is aiming to do the same. Producers are interested mainly in profits, but their products are linked to security risks. This has led to controversial discussions, for example on the role of the Chinese state-owned company Huawei in the 5G roll-out.
> 4) Wherever data are collected they can be misused. That is true for all kinds of data. Nothing comes close to the dimension and speed of this development.

Alongside the definite advantages of the digital transformation – as well as many adaptation problems that go along with any technological transformation – it also means city administrations face a fundamental problem. When municipal services are linked to the use of digital tools, part of the population is excluded – just as those who are illiterate are often left out today. This is, in fact, an abrogation of a city's duties that are, as state institutions, responsible for all their citizens.

Tools that exclude people accept, or even promote, the division of urban society. While all the other problems associated with the digital transformation appear to have solutions, it is unclear how this one can be resolved. Digital hubris, a character trait that is not uncommon among the new middle classes, often makes it difficult to see possible solutions and is just as counterproductive as calls for more digitalization, which have the opposite effect. A really clever solution is needed in order to open up the opportunities inherent to the digital transformation to all of urban society.

A similar problem is intrinsic to the next issue.

6. City and countryside

Would it be an exaggeration to predict the end of the village? For most of human history, the village was the best solution for securing survival. The majority of people therefore lived in villages, where everyone knew everyone else.

More people now live in urban areas, and their number continues to rise. Simultaneously, the differences between urban and rural areas are increasing exponentially. This has led to a curious contradiction. The number of people in farming is steadily decreasing, for which the industrialization of agriculture is partly to blame. And rural life is becoming more and more similar to urban life, with its division of labour and the use of modern technologies, from the automobile to the internet.

On the other hand, the knowledge economy is concentrated in the city and is drawing in many people, putting even more pressure on rural areas. Unlike urban areas, "rural areas, which suffer from the flight of their young and qualified population, thus become steadily more unattractive and steadily lose their function as supplier."[96]

Rural areas are haemorrhaging life – and mounting their very own fightback. This conflict is most extreme in politics where, as for example in the USA, "anti-elite" forces are gaining traction and important offices. *Donald Trump*'s rise to the presidency is one of the clearest examples of this trend. One of the results of this is that social divisions are mirrored in spatial divisions. After the COVID-19 pandemic broke out in 2019, this also became a physical division in places: some rural districts closed their borders to people from the cities. The Chinese government has taken perhaps the most radical approach and plans to urbanize the entire country. For most countries, this is not a viable solution. But at least the problem has been recognized and has sparked knowledgeable debates. The challenge now is to redefine the relationship between the city and the countryside and to find a solution in which all interests are reconciled.[97] First steps in this direction are encouraging, and include a variety of approaches, ideas, and projects.

But just as the city has to forge a new relationship to the countryside, it also has to redefine its role in the world.

7. City and world

What is the city's place in the world? For urbanists, the answer is clear: within a state, it is a territory and a sovereign regional administrative body that sits below the national and federal state level (*Figure 14*).

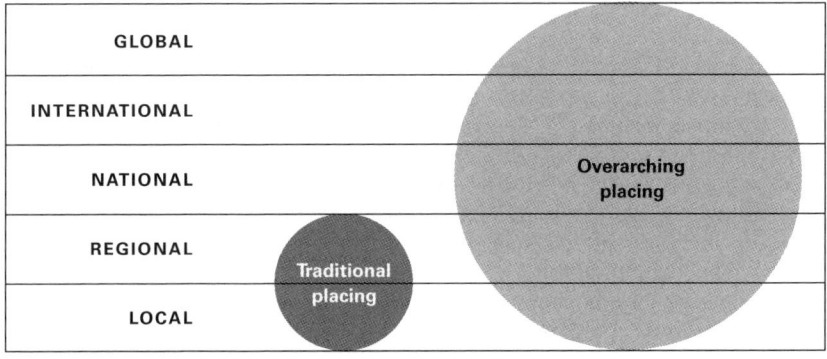

Figure 14. The city in the multi-level model.

---

96   Reckwitz, Andreas (2019), p. 296.
97   Willisch, Andreas (2008). Die Zukunft des Dorfes: Produktionszonen und periphere Menschen, in: Rehberg, Karl-Siegbert (ed.) (2008), Die Natur der Gesellschaft. Frankfurt a.M., p. 577–591.

Figure 15. The city within overlapping segments.

Those who research *international relations* have a hard time determining the city's place. The concept of the *global city*, for instance, does not sit easily with the idea that is inherent to the field, namely that nation-states still play an important role. Models in which these levels overlap have no room for the global city. Because the global city affects all areas of life, there is no place for it within a multilevel system. An attempt to do so results in accounts that clarify nothing.

If the multilevel approach no longer reflects the modern city, then it is time for a new concept. It could place the city at its centre. If we understand the different levels as segments that interact, then it helps us to a) embed the city within a context, b) illustrate different depths, strengths, and ranges of influence, and c) show how the segments in part overlap, as they do in reality. This model resolves the problem of the multilevel approach and is closer to reality, but no more complex (*Figure 15*).

This description is an attempt to do justice to the interactions and dynamics of the 21st century. These run the gamut from economic dependencies and global production and distribution networks to global financial markets that respond on a second by second basis to all kinds of trends that can be found across the world.

That means the city takes on a new role, with new dependencies and new opportunities. Some developments, like *globalization* and the digital transformation, are so powerful that they take root in all cities. They also make it possible for cities to have an influence well beyond their own borders. That has to some extent always been the case, but currently these developments have reached dimensions that amount to a qualitative revolution. Cities now sometimes exhibit features that were previously the sole realm of nation-states and *international relations*.

The last and, in the long run, most important issue we will turn to looks at the new dimensions and their existential meaning for the city.

My personal top 10 cities

1) *Berlin (West), Germany 1945–90*
After the "raisin bombers", silence. Later, a stroll through the city ends at the Wall. "The cities of Berlin" (Uwe Johnson). The half-city of Berlin (West), unwilling to be a political pawn, rose to the status of subject in a historical moment. "We can be heroes | Just for one day." (David Bowie)

2) *Pitigliano, Italy*
A time capsule in tuff. Outside, motionless cliffs; teeming with life within. Calmly it puts up with all the people. Far enough away from Instagrammable hotspots. A glass of unruly pitiglio on a steamy piazza after a summer rain. A perfect moment.

3) *Detroit, USA*
Frosty January winds. One light shining from the top of Book Tower. Gardens in the middle of the block. Restaurants advertize their fare as "Made in Detroit". Vegetables, fish, and meat from the *Eastern Market* are taking the city by storm. Dazzlingly original cocktails in Motown. Detroit's reawakening – one of the wonders of our age.

4) *Marrakesh, Morocco*
Mocha on a sleepy afternoon. My attempt to tell the butcher what I want ends in a hearty laugh. Then he switches to German; he spent 35 years working as a refuse collector in Gelsenkirchen. He picks out a selection of his wurst and gives me a tour of the market. Marrakesh – a city that smiles.

5) *Lhasa, Tibet*
Red vs yellow. Conflicts, battles – not as peaceful as it seems. Underground grumbling. Anti-colonialist … with the exception of the streets. And the forestation. And the schools. And the trains. In a side street, a sign in German: "Kaffee und Kuchen" – coffee and cake.

6) *Sharija, United Arab Emirates*
Backstage in Dubai, in the shadow of the glittering high-rises. Dozens of workers spill out of a minibus, sit on the roof, take a breather. Laundry is washed, people cook, make love. On holidays you can get *Black Forest gateau* from the Pakistani baker around the corner.

7) *Bukhara, Uzbekistan*
When the sun sets over the city square, the restaurants change their drinks menus. The city of historical moments leans back with a cold drink and tells its stories.

8) *St. Petersburg, Russia*
For 8 May, the military bombs a hole in the clouds over the city that feels a lot like Leningrad. The sun burns down, the humidity is tropical. Two bottles of vodka per person held between the knees at 9 a.m. … then the parade.

9) *Washington D.C., USA*
A couple of blocks from the Loop and its venerable political, cultural, and historical institutions – another Washington. *Kramer Books* at *Dupont Circle*; cafés, the stores in *Adams Morgan* – this is where the city of headlines goes calmly about its business.

10) *Sintra, Portugal*
The last tourist bus leaves at 6 p.m. on the dot. Exhale. The locals step out the door, nod at one another, raise a glass, drink, and enjoy the silence for a moment. Now it is their city.

8. City and environment

The city sits solidly, heavily, taking up space in the environment, as urban geographers have fittingly established. The first known use of the word "environment" was in around 1800. It comes from the Danish *omverden*, meaning "the surrounding land, the surrounding world". The environment is more than its related terms "ecosystem" and "nature". While all of these terms have no need of any reference to humans, they are part of the environment, as can be seen in an early definition from 1909: "the surroundings of a living creature, which affects them and their living conditions."[98]

The same can be said of the city. The environment influences the city and to some degree determines its life; conversely, the city also affects the environment. The latter fact is currently one of the biggest problems we face, and is attracting ever greater attention. This development impacts all areas: the soil and its resources, sweet and salt water, the air and its quality, as well as the climate and weather. In-depth research has been conducted in all of these areas and scientists are in almost total agreement that human-made climate change poses an existential threat. Even large companies are adapting to a changing future. Munich Re is one example: "Climate change represents one of the greatest long-term risks of change for the insurance industry. We expect climate change to lead to a lasting increase in extreme weather events."[99]

All the studies and prognoses come to the same conclusion regarding the city: "Cities are at the forefront of climate change. More than half of the global population lives in urban centres, and most economic activities and energy-related emissions are also concentrated there."[100] As a result of climate change, cities by or near the sea may be flooded, or even disappear. Heat and poor-quality air are already making life in many urban areas almost unbearable. While there are plans for countermeasures and adaptation concepts, they are slow in being implemented. Many of these measures require international cooperation, which is increasingly difficult because of states' growing self-centredness. The COVID-19 pandemic of all things has shown how quickly change can come. Global air traffic and industrial production both dropped significantly, as did their respective emissions. At the same time, the associated recession led to a reduction in quality of life and even existential crises. There is no solution in sight that is able to satisfy all the relevant interests and bring about all the necessary changes.

---

98 en.wikipedia.org/wiki/Umwelt (accessed: 23 Apr. 2022).
99 Munich Re, Group Annual Report 2018, www.munichre.com/content/dam/munichre/contentlounge/website-pieces/documents/302-09122.pdf/_jcr_content/renditions/original./302-09122.pdf (accessed: 22 Apr. 2022).
100 Klimafakten.de/sites/default/files/images/reports/graphics/klimawandelundstaedte-web.pdf. See also elib.uni-stuttgart.de/handle/11682/9838 (both accessed: 23 Apr. 2022).

9. Diversity and reciprocities

Issues impact cities and cities impact issues. The examples addressed in the above are currently being discussed passionately, but they are only a part of all the issues affecting cities. None of these issues is fundamentally tied to the city, but they are often particularly prevalent there. They are characterized not only by their dimension, but also by reciprocities. For one, many of these issues are interconnected. They influence one another. Society cannot be meaningfully discussed without looking at the economy, lifestyle, and housing etc. No activity is without consequences for other areas. To discuss these issues, it is always necessary to look beyond subject boundaries and to take all impacts into consideration.

And then there are some issues that are very powerful and all-pervasive. Right now, the big game changers are *globalization*, the digital transformation, and climate change.

To put some order into these many topics, terms, concepts, and city types prioritize different issues. This makes them easier to deal with but, as we saw in the previous chapter, runs the risk of overlooking important influences. In light of the continual growth in urbanization, the consequences can be enormous, and consequential costs often outweigh the promised advantages of an action. That is perhaps the most important insight that an introductory study can proffer. The old method of prioritizing cities according to types, which goes back to *Max Weber*, has become questionable. And so, when examining urban issues, it is important to above all take their great diversity into account and to look for reciprocities. This is a Herculean task for a discipline-oriented academic world.

V. OUR FUTURE WILL BE DECIDED IN AND WITH THE CITY

If the city is the answer, then what is the question? To frame it we first, in a theory section, looked at what research is being conducted in different academic disciplines, at the relevant experts, and then the meanings of the word itself. Based on that we created a theoretical construct with five features: *The city can be understood as creative, densified diversity within a structured unit.*

The form of the city

That describes the city as a form. To be a city, a place has to have *diversity* and an *infrastructure*. What is more, the city is a *unit*, whether administrative, economic, or geographical, to name just a few possibilities. These three characteristics must be present in order to be able to call a place a city, but they do not yet differentiate the city from a village or a country. These, too, are units that have an infrastructure, and they can be diverse. The feature unique to the city is *densification*, or a large number of people living in a relatively small space. That differentiates the city from other forms of living together, for example in a state or a federation.

The Janus face of action within the city

Form provides a framework for human activity, and people's actions shape the forms. People live, work, shop, and engage in recreational activities, that is if they actually have any leisure time. Most of these activities are naturally *efficient*, *timely*, and *routine*. Here, too, there is no difference between urban and rural areas.

(i) Creative action in the city

To illustrate creative urban activity, let us imagine that two densely settled areas are separated by a river. There are many possible ways of connecting them: with a ferry, by building a bridge, flying over it, or digging a tunnel under it. Which of these solutions is appropriate depends on the available technical possibilities, resources, and on other conditions. Based on today's standards, a simple reinforced concrete bridge could be the most common solution. That would not, however, be a creative solution. But the situation was completely different when the first known stone bridge was built over the Euphrates to connect the new city in the west to the huge temple complex of ancient *Babylon* in the east. That first stone bridge was a very creative solution: it was new, surprising, and *established a trailblazing method* as the new standard.[101]

When actions are not routine, *new* and innovative, surprising and *pathbreaking* – in a word, *creative* – solutions are needed. Creative actions can, of course, be found everywhere. Individuals can find new solutions to problems in

---

101 Remains of the bridge were found during German archaeological expeditions in the early 20th century. See Marzahn, Joachim; Schauerte, Günther (2008), Babylon. Mythos und Wahrheit. Munich, p. 75. In antiquity, the bridge, at 123-metres long, was considered one of the (non-canonical) wonders of the world. Eisele, Petra (2006, original 1980), Babylon. Götterpforte oder Große Hure. Düsseldorf, p. 114.

both the city and the countryside. But creative action varies when solutions are being sought that individual people cannot deal with.

Cities are the typical solutions. Their density creates new challenges that in turn elicit new answers. Often these answers are so powerful that they not only change an individual city, but also have an impact far beyond its borders.

It is not easy to evaluate these responses. For a very long time, they were evaluated together and considered to be "progress" and there were good arguments for viewing them positively. A case in point are the many examples of technologies linked to cities, from medicine to electrification, and to the digital transformation. However, considering the recent momentum that global urbanization has gained, we may well now be reaching a point at which the risks outweigh the advantages.

New answers to new questions

The first cities were a regional response to a regional problem. Later, they were understood as a tool for achieving a good life. These motives still exist today. At the same time, we are faced with risks that are larger than any previous dangers. If this is a result of modernity, then we can understand why the philosopher *Jean-François Lyotard* called for the grand narratives to be renounced and why, to this day, his diagnosis meets with such a great response. It leads, for example, to an argument put forward by the philosopher *Susan Neiman*:

> It is time to decide whether we cannot embrace modernity after all – with its possibilities for self-criticism and for change. This entails neither regressing into nostalgia for a premodern age ("Everything was better long ago, today we're decadent.") nor embracing the indifference of postmodernity ("Decadence is just a category like any other that we've already deconstructed."). We have three choices: to mourn premodernity, to greet postmodernity with a yawn, or to continue on the path of modernity with a critical eye. The latter is the only path that allows us to hope for progress of any kind.[102]

The critical continuation of modernity – that sounds a little like whistling loudly in the dark. If the grand narratives are no longer useful, what remains are small stories.

That is a fairly good description of the state of urbanism research. There is an infinite number of wonderful and fascinating viewpoints, but they do not come together to form a coherent image and are therefore difficult to evaluate. Interdisciplinarity may not be the answer to every problem, but it takes us a decisive step further. This introduction to urbanism has been an attempt to illustrate and utilize its potential. Urban features and their interconnections form a

---

[102] Neiman, Susan (2016), Die Quellen allen Unglücks? In: *DIE ZEIT*, 27 Oct. 2016. See also Lyotard, Jean-François (1995), Toward the Postmodern. New Jersey.

matrix of criteria that orders heterogeneous characteristics, allowing us to see connections and the bigger picture.

Perhaps this could also be an answer to the despair with modernity, which cities had a big hand in creating. The city has shaped modernity – and modernity has shaped the city. If the city is still the best tool for increasing collective human potential, then one of the most gripping questions of the present remains how we define the city and what role we want to give the city when it comes to shaping our future. And that would be a grand narrative. Because the future will be decided in and with the city.

Postscript

Does time pass, or does it expire? That is a question of perspective. At any rate, it was not easy to research the city and cities in a time of general crises, including, as my research came to an end, the COVID-19 pandemic. Times like these hone our powers of observation; questions gain in urgency, and answers become more pointed.

The most pressing question is that of relevance. It reveals the gaps in our knowledge, which are, of course, also present in this book. Although its scope is universal, some cultures are missing or are dealt with only in the margins, particularly those in India, Africa, and Australia. That is a shortcoming of this study. But it would not do justice to the subject at hand to subsume cultural specificities under city types. This topic will, therefore, have to be the subject of future research, as will the repositioning of the city within the framework of international relations. Nevertheless, I hope that the ideas presented here help readers to see the city more clearly.

I would like to mention two further aspects that are close to my heart: the connection between theory and practice, and the question of the independence of research, which is always also a question of time and money.

Following the maxim that nothing is more practical than a good theory, I believe that theory has to explain reality so that we can better understand it and thus improve our actions accordingly. For that reason, it was important to me to visit the cities I wrote about whenever possible. Around 100 cities are named in this book. I was able to spend time in almost half of those that still exist. Some places I visited only for a few days; a handful of them I visited for several months at a time. Besides *Berlin*, I also have homes in *Pitigliano* and *Washington D.C.*, all of them cities that can easily be navigated without outside help, by foot and by public transportation.

Research without third-party funding is effectively a thing of the past. There are those who decry this fact, because it creates dependencies, but they are fighting a losing battle. There is no sense in raging against the sea. It is, of course, possible to go one's own way and finance a study completely independently. That is how the study at hand was done and the monetary value of this work – not counting the hours worked – is equal to a midsize luxury sedan. No outside money was put into this work and thus also no external interests. That also answers the question of responsibility: any errors and mistakes are the author's sole responsibility.

Acknowledgements

I would like to thank Detlef Lehnert for his critical reading and his inspiring arguments. Stefalina Midialkou researched the websites of cities across the globe. Frank Odening managed to convert my ideas into persuasive graphics. Ulrike Weingärtner from Text-Akzente competently and carefully edited the German text. And I am also grateful to Sarah Rögl for seeing the book through publication.

Figures and tables

Frank Odening designed all the icons as well as the figures on pages 13, 79, 125, and 126. Figure 8: German Federal Archive, image 146-1986-029-02/1986-029-02; Figure 9: Pedro França/Agência Senado; Figure 2: Wolfgang Sauber; Figure 3: Reinhard Dietrich. All other figures are by the author (p. 15, 55, 61, 69, 102, 110, 119, and 127). It was not possible to find or contact all the rightholders, which is why the author requests that they contact him: uweprell@gmx.de. The tables were created by the author. Tables 1, 2, 5, and 9 as well as the information on p. # are updates of earlier books: Prell, Uwe (2016), Theorie der Stadt in der Moderne: Kreative Verdichtung. Opladen; and Prell, Uwe (2017), Die Stadt: zwölf Sprachen – fünf Bedeutungen. Ein Beitrag zur Theorie der Stadt. Opladen.

Literature

It is impossible to gain a comprehensive overview of all the literature on the city, which covers more than a dozen disciplines. The following bibliography is a combination of the most discussed and influential texts. It includes both classic texts and new works that have acted as forceful catalysts for debate. A guide to more comprehensive reading can be found in Prell, Uwe (2016), Theorie der Stadt in der Moderne. Kreative Verdichtung. Opladen, Berlin, Toronto; and Prell, Uwe (2017), Die Stadt: zwölf Sprachen – fünf Bedeutungen. Ein Beitrag zur Theorie der Stadt. Opladen, Berlin, Toronto.

All the books in the literature list are readily available in libraries, with the exception of the legendary *Handwörterbuch der Soziologie*, published in 1931, which can be bought new or used and is in parts available in digital form. The internet has become an invaluable research tool. In many cases, for example digital encyclopaedias and dictionaries, it provides access to trustworthy sources. But it also has two serious shortcomings. For one, the digitization of analogue sources is not always reliable, and not all sources remain permanently available. For that reason, all digital sources used here were archived in PDF format.

The following 50 titles are my personal quintessence of urban literature. The fact that not all of them deal directly with the city has to do with the complexity of the subject matter.

Amin, Ash; Graham, Stephen (1997), The Ordinary City. Transactions of the Institute of British Geographers, p. 411–429.
Assmann, Ulrike; Born, Lukas; Kochendörfer, Bernd; Pahl-Weber, Elke; Zehner, Carsten (eds.) (2014), Future Megacities. Berlin. Vol. 1: Energy and Sun, Vol. 2: Mobility and Transportation, Vol. 3: Capacity Development, Vol. 4: Local Action and Participation: Space, Planning, and Design.
Barber, Benjamin R. (2013), If Mayors ruled the world. Dysfunctional Nations, rising Cities. New Heaven, London.
Bourdieu, Pierre (1982, original 1979), Die feinen Unterschiede. Kritik der gesellschaftlichen Urteilskraft. Frankfurt a.M.
Bronger, Dirk (2004), Metropolen, Megastädte, Global Cities. Die Metropolisierung der Erde. Darmstadt.
Castells, Manuel (1996–1998), The Information Age: Economy, Society, and Culture. Oxford, Malden MA. | Vol. 1 (1996), The Rise of the Network Society. | Vol. 2 (1997), The Power of Identity. | Vol. 3 (1998). End of Millennium.
Davis, Mike (2007, original 2006), Planet der Slums. Berlin.

Deakin, Mark; Mora, Luca (2019), Untangling Smart Cities. From Utopian Dreams to Innovation Systems for a Technology-Enabled Urban Sustainability. Amsterdam.

Dilcher, Gerhard (1999), Stadtrecht, in: Bader, Karl Siegfried; Dilcher, Gerhard (eds.) (1999), Deutsche Rechtsgeschichte. Land und Stadt – Bürger und Bauer im Alten Europa. Berlin, Heidelberg, New York, p. 1863.

Frey, Oliver; Koch, Florian (eds.) (2011), Positionen zur Urbanistik I. Stadtkultur und neue Methoden der Stadtforschung. Positionen zur Urbanistik II. Gesellschaft, Governance, Gestaltung. Vienna, Berlin.

Friedrichs, Jürgen (1977), Stadtanalyse. Soziale und räumliche Organisation der Gesellschaft. Reinbek.

Glaeser, Edward (2011), Triumph of the City. How urban spaces make us human. London.

Hackworth, Jason (2007), The Neoliberal City. Governance, Ideology, and Development in American Urbanism. New York City.

Heinrich, Klaus (2015), Dahlemer Vorlesungen – Karl Friedrich Schinkel/Albert Speer. Arch+, ed. 219, 20.07.2015.

Hoffmann-Axthelm, Dieter (1993), Die dritte Stadt. Frankfurt a.M.

Jacobs, Jane (2015, original 1961), Tod und Leben großer amerikanischer Städte. Gütersloh, Berlin.

Joas, Hans (1996, original 1992), Die Kreativität des Handelns. Frankfurt a.M.

Johanek, Peter; Post, Franz-Joseph (eds.) (2004), Vielerlei Städte. Der Stadtbegriff. Köln, Weimar, Vienna.

Krastev, Ivan; Holmes, Stephan (2019), Das Licht, das erlosch. Eine Abrechnung. Berlin.

Lefebvre, Henri (1968), Le droit à la ville. Paris.

Lichtenberger, Elisabeth (2002), Die Stadt. Von der Polis zur Metropolis. Darmstadt.

Ljungkvist, Kristin (2016), The Global City 2.0. From strategic site to global actor. London, New York City.

Lyotard, Jean-François (1995), Toward the Postmodern. New Jersey.

Mann, Michel (1994, Original 1986), Geschichte der Macht. Vol. 1. Von den Anfängen bis zur Griechischen Antike. Frankfurt a. M., New York.

Mills, Edwin; Hamilton, Bruce W. (1994), Urban Economics. New Jersey.

Mossberger, Karen; Clarke Susan E.; John, Peter (eds.) (2012), The Oxford Handbook of Urban Politics. New York.

Mumford, Lewis (1963, original 1961), Die Geschichte der Stadt. Köln, Berlin.

Nassehi, Armin (2019), Muster. Theorie der digitalen Gesellschaft. München.

Naßmacher, Hiltrud; Naßmacher, Karl-Heinz (1999), Kommunalpolitik in Deutschland. Opladen.

Nissen, Hans J. (2012), Geschichte Altvorderasiens. München.

Noller, Peter (1999), Globalisierung, Stadträume und Lebensstile. Kulturelle und lokale Repräsentationen des globalen Raums. Opladen.

Oswald, Philipp (ed.) (2005), Schrumpfende Städte. Vol. 1 and 2. Berlin.

Park, Robert Ezra; Burgess, Ernest Watson (1992, original 1925), The City. Suggestions for Investigation of Human Behaviour in the Urban Environment. Chicago, London.

Packer, Georg (2014, original 2013), Die Abwicklung. Eine innere Geschichte des neuen Amerika. Frankfurt a.M.

Paddison, Ronan; Timberlake, Michael (eds.) (2010), Urban Studies. Economy. Los Angeles, London, New Delhi, Singapore, Washington DC. Vol. I: What are Cities? – Vol. II: The Urban Economy – Vol. III: Connected Cities – Hinterlands, Hierarchies, Networks and Beyond – Vol. IV: Political Economy of Real Estate – Social and Political Aspects of Urban Development.

Paddison, Ronan; Ostendorf, Wim (eds.) (2010), Urban Studies. Society. Los Angeles, London, New Delhi, Singapore, Washington DC. Vol. I: Cities as Social Spaces – Vol. II: Experience the City – Vol. III: Designing and Planning Cities – Vol. IV: Cities, Ideas and Ideals

Posener, Julius (1978–83), Vorlesungen I–V. Arch+ eds. 48 (1.12.1979), 53 (1.9.1980), 59 (1.10.1981), 63/64 (1.7.1982), 69/70 (1.8.1983).

Preuss, Hugo (1906), Die Entwicklung des deutschen Städtewesens. Vol. 1: Entwicklung des deutschen Städtewesens. Leipzig.

Reckwitz, Andreas (2019), Das Ende der Illusionen. Politik, Ökonomie und Kultur in der Spätmoderne. Berlin.

Richardson, Henry W.; Nam, Chang Woon (eds.) (2014), Shrinking Cities. New York.

Rink, Dieter; Haase, Annegret (eds.) (2018), Handbuch Stadtkonzepte. Analysen, Diagnosen, Kritiken und Visionen. Opladen, Toronto.

Rolf, Jan Hauke (2006), Urbane Globalisierung. Bedeutung und Wandel der Stadt im Globalisierungsprozess. Wiesbaden.

Sassen, Saskia (1991), The Global City: New York, London, Tokyo. Princeton.

Saunders, Doug (2011), Arrival City. München.

Schäfer, Michael (2014), Kommunalwirtschaft. Eine gesellschaftspolitische und volkswirtschaftliche Analyse. Wiesbaden.

Scott, Alen J. (2001), Global City-Regions. Trends, Theory, Policy. Oxford.

Simmel, Georg (1984, original 1903), Die Großstädte und das Geistesleben, in: Simmel, Georg, Das Individuum und die Freiheit. Berlin, p. 192–204.

Sitte, Camillo (2002, original 1889), Der Städtebau nach seinen künstlerischen Grundsätzen. Wien.

Sombart, Werner (1931), Siedlungen. II. Städtische Siedlung. Stadt, in: Vierkandt, Alfred (ed.), Handwörterbuch der Soziologie. Stuttgart, p. 527–532.

Weber, Max (2000, original 1922), Studienausgabe der Max Weber Gesamtausgabe. Abt. I. Schriften und Reden. Vol. 22. Wirtschaft und Gesellschaft: die Wirtschaft und die gesellschaftlichen Ordnungen und Mächte; Nachlass Teilband. 5. Die Stadt. Edited by Winfried Nippel. Tübingen.

Index

Africa 60, 69, 71, 85, 101, 134
Agriculture 25, 40, 44, 45, 65, 66, 70, 73, 74, 120, 124
Antiquity, ancient city 13, 15, 29, 32, 41, 46, 52, 55, 59, 61, 63, 68, 91, 108, 118, 131
Arabic 10, 13, 14, 60, 70, 71, 76, 77, 102
Archaeology 5, 17, 31, 41, 131
Architecture 9, 17, 20, 26–30, 37, 41, 44, 90, 91
Arrival city 10, 81, 85, 93–96, 107, 111, 112–115
Asia 13, 60, 71, 85, 101
Athens Charter 20, 27, 31, 61
Autonomy 32, 41, 45, 61–63, 65, 74

Bengali 60, 121
Bicycle city 122

Capital city 7, 10, 20 30, 35, 47, 48, 54, 59 63, 65, 70, 72–74, 81, 88, 89, 90, 91, 92, 93, 95, 97, 101, 104, 107, 108, 112–115, 120
Capitalism 20, 35, 47, 48, 59, 108, 120
Car-friendly city 27, 79, 121
Centre 10, 11, 15, 21, 23, 29, 34, 40, 41, 45, 51–53, 58, 61, 63–68, 70–76, 85, 88, 90–92, 100, 107–109, 115–119, 122, 123, 126, 128
Chicago School 9, 19, 20, 46, 47, 49
Chinese 10, 60, 72, 73, 75–77, 104, 124, 125
CIAM 27, 28
Citizens, civil society 9, 19, 21, 22, 29, 41, 55, 61–65, 68, 77, 95, 97, 99, 104, 124
City types 6, 9–11, 15, 38, 39, 45, 57, 63, 65, 66, 79, 80–82, 88, 93, 107, 109, 111–116, 129, 134

Civic empowerment 54
Civilization 10, 14, 42, 43, 46, 59, 70, 71, 77, 93
Climate, climate change 5, 9, 13, 24, 26, 44, 90, 98, 104, 114, 117, 124, 128, 129
Cold War 7, 12, 28, 30, 93, 100, 108
Community 19, 22, 28, 29, 34, 44, 48, 62, 64, 74, 123
Creativity 53, 54, 55, 77, 78, 80, 85, 87, 90, 95, 99, 103, 105, 106, 109, 113, 114

Danube Valley civilization 59
Democracy 54
Density 10, 13, 14, 21, 22, 24, 46, 37, 39, 40, 42, 44, 46–48, 53, 55, 58, 65–69, 73–75, 77, 84, 107, 115, 121, 132
Digitalization, digital transformation 5, 10, 20, 21, 33, 47, 52, 53, 79, 80, 86, 88, 90, 98, 99, 102, 103, 123, 124, 126, 129, 132, 135, 136
Diversity 10, 13, 14, 22, 31, 36, 37 39, 40, 41, 44, 45, 52, 53, 57, 58, 61, 65, 71, 72, 74–76, 80, 84–86, 87, 92, 93, 94, 95, 99, 103, 105, 106, 109, 113, 114, 116, 129, 131
Divided city 87, 88, 106
Dual city 87, 88

Economics, economy 5, 6, 9, 10, 12, 17, 20, 22, 23–25, 37, 39, 40, 44, 48, 51, 52, 54, 58, 66–68, 70, 72, 73, 74, 77, 80, 81, 84, 85, 86, 88, 95, 100, 101, 103, 112, 115, 118, 119, 120, 129, 135, 136
Egyptian 9, 13, 59, 60, 61, 77, 91
English 7, 26, 59, 67, 68, 72, 76, 77, 102, 104, 122

138

Environment, environmental pollution 5, 9, 10, 24, 26, 47, 49, 68, 80 81, 85, 98, 104, 115, 117, 121, 122, 128

Fertile Crescent 13–15
France, French 10, 29, 30, 60, 66–68, 71, 75, 77, 102

Gentrification 54, 119
Geography 9,, 12, 17, 24–27, 37, 40
German 7, 10, 22, 23, 25, 27–31, 34, 55, 60, 68, 75, 76, 77, 84, 88, 90, 91, 99, 102, 108, 119, 120, 127, 131, 134, 135
Global city 9–11, 12, 19, 20, 21, 34, 38, 39, 42, 50–54, 54, 67, 81, 84, 85, 86, 88, 104, 111, 112, 114, 115, 126, 128
Globalization 23, 34, 39, 51, 52, 86, 87, 90, 107, 119, 126, 129
Governance 18, 19, 21, 37, 42, 51, 54, 97, 101,
Greece, Greek 9, 43, 46, 63, 101, 103

Heterogeneity 48, 53, 54, 57, 75
Hindi 10, 55, 60, 71–73, 76, 77
History 6, 9, 12, 13, 15, 18,22, 30–32, 41, 46, 55, 67, 82, 93, 104, 108, 123, 124

Immigration 10, 81, 86, 94, 96, 116, 117
Industry, industrialization 11, 15, 27, 32, 42, 47, 48, 51, 52, 66, 67, 70, 72, 74, 81, 85, 87, 88, 88, 96, 100, 108, 109, 119, 120, 122–124, 128
Infrastructure 15, 24, 39, 41, 61, 76, 77, 79, 85–87, 90, 92, 93, 95, 97, 99 103–106, 109, 113, 114, 117, 122, 123, 131

Innovation, innovative 11, 12, 17, 24, 30, 31, 40, 49, 51, 52, 62, 66, 78, 80, 81, 98, 100, 102, 110, 131
International, International relations 19, 21, 24, 28, 30, 34, 38, 41, 50, 52, 67, 70, 88, 110, 125, 126, 128, 134
Islam, Islamic city 33, 71, 90

Japan, Japanese 60, 66, 70, 71, 73–77, 89, 108

Language, philosophy of language 6, 7, 9, 12, 58–61, 63, 68, 70–72, 75–78, 84, 120,
Large settlement, big city 14, 15, 23, 42, 45, 46–48, 68, 75
Latin 9, 18, 59, 60, 63–66, 68, 71, 75–77
Latin America 60, 101
Levels 18, 19, 22, 26, 35, 36, 39–42, 53, 74, 79, 81, 89, 92, 99, 105, 116, 120, 121, 125, 126,
Linguistics 58, 59, 65, 96
Lost city 10, 82, 107, 111–115

Mandarin 72, 73, 102
Market 9, 23, 24, 32, 39, 41, 345, 48, 50–52, 57, 61, 68, 73, 81, 86, 87, 97, 98, 100, 101, 103, 104, 106, 107, 110, 113, 118–120, 124, 126, 127
Mayor 34, 55, 79, 135
Megacity 10, 81–86, 112, 114, 115
Mesopotamia 59
Metropolis 19, 25, 51, 65, 72, 84, 110, 118
Middle Ages 29, 32, 52, 66, 68, 118, 124
Municipal politics 17, 23, 24, 28, 29, 32, 34–37, 39, 41, 42, 55, 64, 65, 68, 85, 89, 95, 99, 118, 122–124

Neoliberalism, neoliberal city 10, 23, 103, 104
New urbanism 18

Old city 11, 13, 14, 66,
Open city 9, 56, 57, 107, 111
Ordinary city 9, 52–54
Orient 5, 31,
Philosophy 6, 9, 17, 22, 27, 32–34, 36, 42, 43, 46, 55, 58, 59, 62, 75, 98, 132
Polis 25, 46, 61–65, 68,
Politics, political science 9, 12, 17, 21, 24, 34–37, 42–45, 51, 55, 63, 70, 74, 75, 77, 92, 117, 125,
Population 13, 24, 25, 31, 40, 44–47, 51, 62, 64–68, 70–75, 80–84, 87–89, 94, 95, 99, 100, 105, 106, 108, 109, 115, 116, 122–125, 128
Portugal, Portuguese 60, 127
Post-political city

Residential city 11, 57, 66, 67, 73, 74
Russia, Russian 10, 60, 70, 75–77, 101, 102, 108, 122, 127

Satellite city 66
Shrinking city 10, 52, 81, 82, 107–115, 118
Slum 69, 93–96, 116, 119
Small city 55, 64, 66, 73, 81, 89
Smart city 11, 15, 38, 67, 79, 81, 83, 96–100, 103–112, 114, 115, 121, 123

Social engineering 20, 28
Sociology 6, 9, 12, 17, 19, 20– 22, 33, 36, 37, 39, 43, 46, 50, 51, 76,
Spain, Spanish 60, 65, 68, 71, 75–77, 102
Spatial planning 9, 17, 26-28, 37,
Sustainable city 26, 98, 100, 111, 122

Tool 5, 6, 9, 12, 13, 15, 20, 26, 27, 34, 46, 37, 42, 43, 46, 48, 52, 57, 63, 72, 87, 98-100, 102, 123, 124, 132, 133
Town twinning programme 28

Unit 24, 27, 29, 31, 32, 34, 36, 40, 41, 49, 53, 61, 62, 65, 68, 70–72, 74, 76, 78, 80, 82, 85–88, 93, 95, 99, 1103, 105, 106, 109, 113, 114, 131,
Urban area 73, 110, 111
Urban economics 9, 17, 23, 24, 37, 39
Urban geography 9, 17, 24, 26, 37, 40
Urban morphology 9, 17, 26, 27
Urban planning 9, 12, 17, 20, 26, 27, 38, 41, 56, 57, 97
Urban sprawl 18
Urbanism, urbanity, urbanization 9–10, 17–19, 27, 28, 35, 37, 39, 47, 50, 56, 64, 73, 82, 103, 108, 109, 129, 132

Village 32, 36, 41, 66–68, 70–74, 96, 118, 124, 131
Virus city 10, 82, 104–107, 111–115

Index of cities

Adelaide 102
Akron 121
Aleppo 71
Amsterdam 88, 94, 100, 116, 122
Ashaiman 95
Athens 20, 27, 31, 61
Auckland 116
Awra Amba

Babylon 28, 31, 91, 131
Baghdad 71
Bangalore 122
Barcelona 18, 20, 56, 122
Baghdad
Bengaluru 121
Berlin 12, 18, 19, 30, 46, 52, 55, 69, 73, 90–93, 106, 110, 118, 119, 127, 134
Berlin (West) 30, 69, 127
Bogotá 102, 212
Bratislava 102
Brussels 92, 116
Bukhara 127
Byblos 15

Cádiz 121
Cairo 71
Çatalhöyük 13–15
City of Westminster 67
Constitución 119
Copenhagen 122

Damascus 71, 119
Den Haag 84
Detroit 108–10, 127
Dhaka 119
Dharavi 95
Dubai 90, 116–118, 127

Eridu 15

Fez 71
Florence 52
Frankfurt am Main 116,

Germania 29, 911
Greensboro-High Point 121
Gulf of Khambhat Cultural Complex (GKCC) 13, 14

Hiroshima 108
Hong Kong 88, 122

Jericho 13, 15
Jerusalem 93

Kairouan 71
Karachi 95
Karlsruhe 91
Kinshasa 89
Königsberg 93
Kuala Lumpur 117

Lagos 88, 119
Lhasa 127
Liechtenstein 88
London 50, 57, 67, 69, 88, 104, 116, 117
Los Angeles 94, 102, 116, 118

Manila 88, 121
Marrakesh 127
Marseille 88
Mecca 71, 90
Medellín 122
Medina 71
Melbourne 116, 119
Mexico City 94
Montréal 102
Moscow 89
Mumbai 94, 95

141

Nagasaki 108
Nauru 89
New York City 20, 27, 52, 56, 57, 69, 85, 87, 88, 107, 116, 117

Orangi Town 95

Palau 89
Paris 20, 56, 57, 66, 94, 116
Pitigliano 127, 134
Pompeii 15, 55, 108
Portland 122

Rabat 71
Riga 102
Rome 29, 31, 52, 57, 63, 64, 81, 91

San Marino 89
São Paulo 94
Seoul 88, 89
Shanghai 11, 57, 87, 102
Sharija 127
Singapore 88, 116
Sintra 127
St. Lucia 89

St. Petersburg 127
Stockholm 122
Sydney 116, 117, 119

Tehran 94
Tel Aviv 102
Tell Brak 15
Thessaloniki 102
Tokyo 50, 74, 85, 88, 89
Toronto 116, 117
Tunis 71

Ulm 102
Ur 15
Utrecht 122

Vaduz 89
Vatican City 89, 90
Villa el Salvador 95

Washington D.C. 91, 134
Wuhan 104

Yamoussoukro 90

Index of persons

Amin, Ash 9, 52, 53, 58
Aristotle 9, 21, 32–34, 43, 46, 48, 54, 57, 61, 63, 71, 75
Aravena, Alejandro 119

Bauman, Zygmunt 55
Beck, Ulrich 120
Bloch, Ernst 33
Bowie, David 69
Braudel, Fernand 55, 59
Breasted, James Henry 13
Brinkmann, Melanie 106
Bregović, Goran 69

Calvino, Italo 55
Castells, Manuel 16, 20
Cerdà, Ildefons 18, 20, 56
Cicero 32, 46, 64

Dagerman, Stig 55
Darwin, Charles 25
Davis, Mike 95, 96, 116
Demosthenes 61
Dickens, Charles 96
Dilcher, Gerhard 28, 29
Drosten, Christian 106

Engels, Friedrich 47, 48

Fairchild, Thomas 26
Fichte, Johann Gottlieb 33
Frey, Oliver 18, 19, 27, 136
Friedrichs, Jürgen 9, 21, 49, 50, 57

Gershwin, George 69
Graham, Stephen 9, 52–54, 58
Grimm, Jacob 68
Grimm, Wilhelm 68

Harris, Robert 51
Hegel, Georg Wilhelm Friedrich 33

Heit, Alfred 31
Held, Gerd 53
Hoffmann-Axthelm, Dieter 20, 51
Holmes, Stephen 117

Joas, Hans 77

Kant, Immanuel 31, 33, 55
Kekulé, Alexander 106
Kelsen, Hans 33
Koch, Florian 18, 19, 45
Krastev, Ivan 117

Le Corbusier 27
Lefebvre, Henri 20, 33
Lennon, John 69, 85
Libbe, Jens 96, 97, 100
Lichtenberger, Elisabeth 12, 25
Li Keqiang 73
Lyotard, Jean-François 33, 34, 132

Marley, Bob 69
Marx, Karl 33, 47, 48, 103
Mehta, Suketu 55
Morus, Thomas 33
Mumford, Lewis 20, 22, 25, 55

Naßmacher, Hiltrud & Karl-Heinz
Neubauer, Dirk 55
Nissen, Hans J. 5, 13, 31, 111
Noah, Yuval 6

Orbán, Viktor Mihály 117

Paddison, Ronan 25, 35, 36
Pagano, Michael A. 35
Park, Robert Ezra 19, 39, 47, 49, 95
Plato 33, 43, 61

Radbruch, Gustav 33
Ratzel, Friedrich 25

143

Rawls, John 33
Reckwitz, Andreas 120, 125

Sassen, Saskia 9, 11, 20, 21, 35, 38, 39, 50–53, 58, 86
Saunders, Doug 94–96, 111
Saviano, Roberto 55
Schelsky, Helmut 120
Schipper, Sebastian 101
Schmitt, Carl 33
Sennett, Richard 9, 18, 20, 45–47, 54, 55–58, 64, 100
Simmel, Georg 19, 22, 43, 46–48, 53, 57
Sitte, Camillo 27
Sixtus V 57
Sombart, Werner 6, 9, 22, 31, 32, 39, 44, 45, 47, 48, 57, 60

Sophocles 61
Streeck, Hendrik 106

Trump, Donald 117, 125

vom und zum Stein, Karl Baron 97, 100
von Below, Georg 31, 53
von Schmoller, Gustav 31, 32

Warhol, Andy 85
Weber, Max 9, 19, 22, 23, 25, 31, 32, 39, 43, 45, 46, 47, 48, 52, 57, 58, 110, 129
Wirth, Louis 9, 19, 25, 39, 46–49, 57

Zille, Heinrich 118